When Alcohol Abuses Our Marriage

**Stories of real couples
who saved their marriages**

Recovery of Hope Series

When Alcohol Abuses Our Marriage

Stories of real couples
who saved their marriages

Recovery of Hope Series

Steve Wilke
Dave & Neta Jackson

New Leaf Press

New Leaf Press
First printing: April 1995

ISBN: 0-89221-285-3
Library of Congress Catalog: 94-69840

While the stories in this book are true, the
names and other identifiable details of the
characters have been changed.

Contents

Introduction

At the front door my wife and I gave Danny and Tess a hug, said goodnight, and watched as they headed for their car. As I shut the door, I snuck a glance at Neta. I knew she knew what I was thinking.

"I don't know how many more times I can listen to that story," she confessed. "It's always the same."

"I know." I sighed. As lay pastor of a small group in our church, I often listened as one of the small group members or married couples poured out some crisis that needed prayer or biblical counsel. At first we had gladly welcomed Danny and Tess when they came to share their troubles . . . but soon the refrain sounded suspiciously familiar:

Danny had just quit yet another job (or he'd been fired); the problem was an "unreasonable" boss or an "impossible" coworker; someone had "done him a dirty deal" and he wasn't going to put up with that; besides, Danny had a bigger and better plan that was going to put them on Easy Street within six months.

All the time Danny was talking, Tess would fight back weary tears. She was trying to hang in there with Danny, but she was oh, so tired of trying to manage a household and growing family on promises and dashed hopes. When sharing privately with my wife, she had confided, "I can't take the stress much longer. Sometimes I think divorcing Danny is the only thing that will bring me any peace."

We prayed together. We gave them practical tips on managing stress. We applied to the Deacon's Fund when they needed rent or food. We passed along job openings that came to our attention. We rejoiced when Danny landed THE job that was going to solve all their problems.

But somehow we were never surprised when Danny and Tess showed up on our doorstep once again.

Then one day I went to a pastoral training session on alcohol addiction. As I listened to the speaker talk about people who have unrealistic goals and expectations, who are always blaming someone else when things go wrong, who deny that personal or marital problems are as bad as they seem, who always seem to be playing "mind games" with reality . . . I thought of Danny.

But I had never seen Danny take a drink! And Tess had never mentioned drinking as a problem.

Still, the next time we sat down to talk and pray together I said, "Danny, I would like you to consider going for professional counseling." I outlined some of the symptoms of a "compulsive disorder" similar to alcohol addiction. To my surprise, Danny didn't brush me off.

Not long after that Danny and Tess moved, pursuing yet another job and solution to their troubles. When next we heard from them a few years later, we learned that Danny had gone for professional counseling — and now was confessing that for all 15 years of their marriage, he had been an active alcoholic and drug abuser, a fact he kept secret from everyone, including Tess.

He was now working through a Twelve Step program, owning his problem and working toward solutions.

"It's not peaches and cream yet," wrote Tess. "But at least now we're calling our problems by the right name. That at least gives them a handle and a way to deal with them."

As you read the true stories in this book,

you'll see how other couples grappled with this same insidious enemy that threatened to destroy their marriage. At some point all the couples thought divorce was their only option. How each couple found the courage to name the problem and seek help depended on a critical factor: hope.

Each couple has also participated in Recovery of Hope, a program sponsored by a network of counseling centers around the country. Every day marital conflicts are resolved, hurts healed, brokenness made whole — but most people do not hear about these successes. And because they do not hear the accounts of restored marriages, they have no hope when their own marriage gets in trouble.

The Recovery of Hope Network has helped hundreds of couples recover hope in their marriage primarily by giving them an opportunity to hear other couples, who have been through the worst, tell their stories of reconciliation. The message is clear: With help, marriages can be restored.

Throughout the book and especially in the fourth chapter, Dr. Steve Wilke, a licensed clinical psychologist and former president of Recovery of Hope Network, Inc., provides insights into how alcohol deadens the pain, masks the realities, and otherwise hinders healing. He also highlights the steps that lead to self-awareness and true communication — the prerequisites for re-building a damaged relationship.

Dave and Neta Jackson

Chapter One

Strapped in a Straitjacket

Rosalyn Hansen unbuckled the rear seat belt and lifted the dozing two year old from his car seat. *Rats,* she thought. *Now Luke won't be ready to go to bed after supper.* "C'mon, Cari," she said to the six year old scrambling out of the front seat, "let's see if Daddy's home."

When Rosalyn walked in the front door with Luke slung over her shoulder and Cari pulling on the diaper bag, she realized Daddy was home all right — drunk. Lonny Hansen was sprawled on the couch, staring at the TV with half-closed eyes, a beer can clutched in his hand, and several empties lying on the floor.

"Daddy!" squealed Cari. The little girl ran over to the couch, crawled up onto his chest, and gave him a big kiss under the full brown moustache. Then she slid off and backed away. "Phew, Daddy, you stink."

Familiar anger surged through Rosalyn. "Look at you, Lonny Hansen," she snapped. "Even your kids are disgusted by your drinking."

Lonny waved her away with the beer can. "Aww, Rosalyn. Don' start in on that again. I had a hard day at that stupid factory. Jus' had a few beers to relax when I got home."

"Yeah, right," muttered Rosalyn, marching into the kids' room to change Luke's diaper. "At least it's a job!" she yelled back over her shoulder.

A moment later Lonny appeared in the doorway, leaning his lanky frame against the door jamb. "Wha's that supposed to mean? It's not my fault I got laid off at Chrysler."

Rosalyn unsnapped Luke's outfit, pulled off the rubber pants, and unpinned the soaked diaper. Her movements were rough and Luke started to cry.

"Maybe not," she said tersely. "But you'll be lucky to keep this one if you keep drinking like a fish."

"You watch your mouth, lady!"

Rosalyn heard the shift in tone and knew she shouldn't say anymore. But why should she have to tiptoe around this 27-year-old baby, who needed his beer to get through the day like Luke needed his bottle?

Rosalyn put Luke, still crying, into his crib, then whirled on Lonny in the doorway. "No, I won't watch my mouth! I'm sick of playing second fiddle to a six-pack. I work all day, shop for groceries on the way home, pick up the kids at the babysitter, come home dead tired — and what do I find? A husband who's soused on the couch!"

"Wha's your problem?" Lonny shot back. "I'm home, ain't I? You nag if I stop at the bar; you nag if I come home and enjoy a few —"

"Oh, grow up!"

As she spat out the words, Rosalyn had an urge to laugh hysterically. She was only 24 herself. At 15 she'd met Lonny at the drive-in restaurant where she was a carhop. She'd fallen in love with the dark brown eyes, the wavy brown hair that he wore full and long on his neck, the way he made her feel so grown up and special. After all, he was almost 19 and wise in the ways of the world.

At 16, she got pregnant with Cari; madly in love, she and Lonny decided to get married against her parents' wishes. Rosalyn was sure marriage and a family would help Lonny settle down; he'd quit drinking and they'd live happily ever after.

But it didn't happen that way.

They'd been married for seven years, were trying to buy the little farm they lived on, had another baby — and Lonny still wanted to stop at the bar on the way home from work, hung out with his drinking buddies on the weekend, even stayed out all night if he felt like it. But when Rosalyn got on his case, it was a big fight.

"The problem with you, Rosalyn," Lonny slurred from the doorway, "is you don' want anybody t' have fun. Any time I wanna relax or go have fun with the boys, you ruin it all with your nag, nag, nag."

The control snapped. "Me ruin it all?" she screamed. "You're drunk, you smell like a brewery, you're late coming home half the time, you're a bad example for your kids, you spend more time hot-rodding in your latest truck than you do at home ... and you dare to accuse me of ruining it all?"

Grabbing the diaper bag she'd just unloaded, Rosalyn stuffed fresh diapers and a couple of clean outfits for both kids into it, picked up the wailing toddler from the crib, and pushed past Lonny. The smell of alcohol made her feel like gagging.

He followed her to the bathroom. "Whad'ya think you're doin'?"

"Leaving." Balancing Luke on her hip, she threw her toothbrush, hairbrush, and makeup into the diaper bag and zipped it shut.

"Oh, no, you're not!" Lonny's hand snaked out toward the bag but Rosalyn snatched it out of reach.

"Yes, I am! Get out of my way!" She gave him a shove, and in his unsteady state he stumbled. Dashing out of the bathroom she yelled, "Cari! Where are you?"

The little girl was parked in front of the TV her father had left on. Rosalyn tried to calm her voice. "Come on, honey. We're going bye-bye."

"But I'm hungry, Mommy!"

Supper. Rosalyn had totally forgotten about supper. "We'll — uh — eat at Grandma's, okay, darling?"

With Cari in tow, she started for the front door — only to meet Lonny coming out of their bedroom carrying two of her dresser drawers.

"You wanna leave?" he yelled. "Well, don' forget your clothes!" With that he wrestled the front door open and chucked both drawers into the front yard. Then he went back into the bedroom.

Now Rosalyn was scared. "Quick, Cari, get in the car." She hustled both kids out the door toward the driveway. Behind her another dresser drawer came flying out the door and splintered on the lawn.

Heart pounding, Rosalyn opened the car door, pushed both kids inside and locked all the doors before she strapped Luke in his car seat. The keys! Did she have the keys! Yes . . . she'd dropped both the car keys and her wallet in the bag.

As she stuck the key into the ignition, Rosalyn saw Lonny running toward them. The engine came to life just as he reached the car and grabbed the passenger side door handle. Trying not to panic, Rosalyn put the car in reverse and started to back out of the driveway.

Just then Cari screamed and Rosalyn felt a bump. "Mommy! Daddy fell! You just ran over daddy!"

• • •

At the hospital, Rosalyn sat dejectedly in a chair, holding both Luke and Cari on her lap, while a policeman took a statement from Lonny about what had happened. Lonny lay on a gurney, wincing whenever he moved. An initial examination had showed nothing broken, just several bruised ribs, bruised left shoulder, and badly bruised groin area.

"She ran over you a second time?" the policeman asked, barely controlling a smirk.

"Yeah, well, I guess she was tryin' to get

off me, so then she went forward and the tire went right over my body again."

The policeman turned and looked at Rosalyn. Rosalyn looked away. Then he turned back to the gurney.

"You wanna press charges or anything?"

Rosalyn squeezed her eyes shut against the tears that threatened to flow down. She heard Lonny say, "Nah. It wasn't really her fault. . . ."

She felt terrible for running over Lonny; she was glad he wasn't seriously injured. But . . . the policeman had the gall to ask if he wanted to press charges? That was the last straw! It always seemed to turn out like this. Even though Lonny was the one who got drunk, she was the one who got punished.

• • •

It was hard to see when she was in love, 16, and pregnant, but now Rosalyn realizes her marriage had a lot going against it before it ever began. "Between kindergarten and sixth grade my family moved back and forth between Indiana and California seven times," she says. "Both my parents were alcoholic and never had the time to give me the love and affection I needed."

When her mom and dad went out drinking, they often left Rosalyn and her sisters with their landlord, whom they called

"Grandpa." "I was about five at the time," she recalls, "and he was as close to a grandpa as I ever had. He provided some of the warmth and closeness I craved so much. Sometimes I got to stay all night with him. He would take me out to supper; then he might buy me new shoes and clothes that Mom and Dad could never afford. When we came home he wanted me to take a bath with him — to make sure I was clean, he said. Then we would go to bed together."

These "special times" went on for a long time and Grandpa slowly led little Rosalyn from one thing to the next. "He always told me that the things we did together would be our secret. Because it was so 'secret' I knew it must be wrong," says an older and wiser Rosalyn. "But at the same time I was getting the attention and affection I was so hungry for. I was a very confused little girl."

Rosalyn remembers feeling like a little bird in a cage with a cat clawing at it — wanting out of the cage, yet feeling a kind of security in there. "I was helpless and frightened, secure and loved, all at the same time." At that time Rosalyn started having severe asthma attacks until about age 13, which she now knows were caused by holding so much tension and confusion inside.

As Rosalyn moved into her teen years,

she was still looking for love and affection. She remembers wishing someone would just hold her and tell her how pretty she was "without all the rest" boys thought went with it. Or if only someone could be as caring and gentle as Grandpa had seemed.

"But I also remembered the guilt and fear," she says. "I would go just so far with one boy after another, then get scared and tell them to leave me alone. The hunger for closeness was so strong, it was like being sucked into a funnel cloud, whirling around and around. I went from one boy to the next in search of the love only Grandpa had given me — which I both craved and feared."

Afterwards, Rosalyn remembers, she always felt like a baby whose bottle or security blanket had been taken away. And once during her teen years she even took an overdose of aspirin to try to get rid of the loneliness and feelings of being deserted.

Every gift of life comes with an unwritten understanding: "some assembly required." We are created with needs, such as love, respect, worth, fulfillment, satisfaction, and joy, just to name a few.

In marriages like the Hansens, the assembly is out of whack. Some pieces have been assembled by others, some by themselves, and some jointly. In cycles of dysfunction, each person's desperate attempt for personal survival triggers an even more desperate response by the other. Each flurry of interaction fuels the fire until the pot boils over.

The sheer fatigue of the "eruption" creates a cooling-off phase in which distance, blame, shame, and guilt abound. The calm before the storm only sets up stronger storms. Self-esteem, relational skills, and spiritual well-being are so handicapped by our improper assembly that we cannot stop hurting ourselves and the others around us.

Rosalyn and Lonny weren't seeking despair and destruction. But that's where their drama was heading.

Lonny Hansen wheeled his hot 1969 Roadrunner into an empty space at the drive-in restaurant in Rochester, Indiana, and squinted at the menu board.

"May I take your order?" asked a cheerful voice at the car window.

Lonny turned his head and his heart seemed to jump. The pretty carhop had sun-kissed brown hair tucked into her uniform cap, twinkling brown eyes, creamy white skin, and lips with just a touch of rosy gloss. He continued to stare until she said again, "Do you want to order?"

"Oh! Uh . . . yeah. I'll have a burger with

the works, chocolate shake, and double fries."

"Me, too," piped up his buddy from the passenger side.

The girl repeated the order, then moved to the next car.

Lonny turned to his companion. "Did you see that carhop, man? I'm in love!"

His friend craned his neck and eyed the carhop as she walked toward the restaurant to fill the orders. "Yeah, she's kind of cute," he admitted.

"Kind of!" snorted Lonny. He couldn't believe the feelings tumbling around inside him. "I tell you, man, that's the girl I'm going to marry."

His friend looked at him as if he was crazy. "You're loony, man! She's just a kid — still in school. You don't even know her name."

Lonny just smiled a funny smile. When the carhop came back with their window tray, piled high with burgers, shakes, and fries, he said, "I'm Lonny Hansen. What's your name?"

The girl hesitated. "Rosalyn."

"Rosalyn. That's a beautiful name," Lonny said. "Say, could I come by when you get off work and we could talk or something?"

The girl seemed a little flustered, and flattered, too. "Well, I guess that would be all right. I get off at 11 p.m. Bye. I've got other customers to take care of."

Munching his burger, Lonny couldn't keep his eyes off the carhop named Rosalyn. "It really felt like love at first sight," says Lonny today. "My friend called me a crazy liar . . . but I've never gotten over that feeling."

However, Lonny's relationship with Rosalyn's father was anything but "love at first sight." When 18-year-old Lonny started dating 15-year-old Rosalyn, her dad threatened terrible things he would do with parts of the boy's anatomy if he got her into any trouble. "After about a year, Rosalyn and I realized that the marriage we both wanted so badly — probably for all the wrong reasons — just wasn't going to be possible unless something really drastic happened. Then she became pregnant."

As for Rosalyn, she says, "What mixed feelings! I was still a young girl; he was 19 and a man. Affection had always come from an older man, but I was scared — especially when people told me he was no good. He drank all the time and got picked up by the law. And my dad hated him!

"But from the first time we met, Lonny

told me he loved me so much. And he seemed caring and gentle. So I didn't believe them. How could someone so sweet be no good? I had seen a lot of drinking in my life; unlike my Dad, Lonny was never angry, didn't put me down or call me names."

Lonny's drinking did cause some problems, however. He sometimes passed out in the middle of a date. He often spent his paycheck on Rosalyn instead of paying his bills, at which point his parents would kick him out of the house. And one time he kept her out until 5:00 a.m., and her parents had the cops out looking for them.

But in spite of that, to starry-eyed Rosalyn, Lonny seemed like the man she'd been looking for to give her the love and security she'd gotten before from "Grandpa." "So," she shrugs, "I got pregnant so my folks would let us get married. That first year Lonny only drank occasionally, and except for our wedding night, never got drunk."

Compared to life in each of their own families, the first year of marriage felt pretty good to the two young people. "When our daughter Cari was born I was so happy," says Lonny. "But underneath there was also a lot of fear. Such a big responsibility!"

Shortly after Cari was born the drinking

began again. To a bewildered Rosalyn, "It was like Lonny couldn't handle being tied down. He would come home drunk, or even stay out all night. When I complained about it, he got angry and said things that hurt so bad. One time he said our daughter was the only one he loved, and he couldn't stand me. I felt like trash that had been stomped on before being thrown away."

Lonny couldn't figure out what the fuss was all about; to him, drinking was a natural part of life, like getting a new car every year. "I was surprised when the woman who had agreed to share my life not only wouldn't join me in my drinking parties, but nagged and complained about them. At first I felt angry; then disappointed. It made me feel like she no longer loved me the way she used to.

"I wish I'd stayed with the anger," he says now. "At least that is feeling something. Instead, I stuffed my disappointment and feeling of rejection, and used drinking to keep from feeling hardly anything at all."

Since Rosalyn refused to join Lonny in something he enjoyed, Lonny decided he'd have to find someone else to drink with. That "someone else" turned out to be a woman who shared his love for booze. They went out together for about six months until

Rosalyn found out about it. "Then," in Lonny's words, "all hell broke loose."

Rosalyn nods in agreement. "When I caught my husband with a female drinking buddy, we got into such a fight that I filed assault and battery charges — which of course just led to more fights at home."

It is no wonder that couples have such a hard time with open honesty. The "courting" process usually runs counter to the dynamics of a healthy marriage. While dating, couples have little interest in any information which might burst the bubble. Furthermore, both tend to put their best foot forward and hide all shortcomings.

The wedding day symbolizes the beginning of marriage; the realities of marriage come later. As couples experience who they are in a marriage and who their spouse is, the temptation is to panic, pull away, or try to control.

But conflicted, confused moments are windows of opportunity. Unfortunately, most of us react with anger and blame. This leads to brokenness.

With God's grace, couples need to take these moments of disclosure (as negative as they might be) and respond with a desire to understand. Couples who go through conflict with goals of self-exploration and mutual understanding can find reconciliation and wholeness.

When Rosalyn confronted the other woman and told her it was all over, Lonny felt badly about it. "But I also realized then that I really did love my wife," he says. "I could get along without a drinking partner — but not without the drinking.

Rosalyn's refusal to go drinking with him still hurt, however. "I felt like she had thrown up a wall between us," he says. "So I started putting up a wall of my own. As more of my emotions and feelings went down the drain, I escaped further and further into a kind of nothingness. The wall I built around myself became my safe castle, and I wouldn't let anyone in, not even Rosalyn. It felt safe . . . but it sure was lonely in there."

Rosalyn, too, felt all alone with no one to turn to. "My father said I'd made my choice and I'd just have to live with it." But as Lonny's drinking got worse, he sometimes got physical and she didn't feel safe. "Sometimes I found myself going to the floor to protect my head from being battered," she says. "At first, I put the blame on his drinking buddies for being such a bad influence on him, but gradually my love toward him just vanished. I felt like someone had taken my heart and tied it in knots as tight as they could. Sometimes I felt like I was dangling at the end of a rope, but I couldn't let go because there wasn't any place to fall."

So Rosalyn just hung on. "I was a great controller," she admits, "so I kept trying to 'fix things up.' I judged everything Lonny did and hounded him about how great he could be if he would just quit drinking. Then I thought, *If I get pregnant again, that might help . . . like when we first got married.* So I did, even though Lonny kept saying he didn't have enough love in his heart for another child. And, sure enough, Luke's birth only made matters worse. The more I tried to 'fix' things, the worse everything seemed to get for both of us."

Lonny knew Rosalyn thought his drinking would ease up when they had another baby. "But I drank all the more," he admits, "because I really didn't want the responsibility. I thought a baby would interfere with my drinking. I was right; it did. At least, I felt more guilty about drinking."

Even with two kids, the pretty young carhop (now 21 and working as a hospital dietitian) could still turn heads. "Lonny was so jealous," she recalls. "He didn't like to take me places for fear I would get attention from other men. The fact was, he was still angry at me for not going drinking with him. So when he came home he acted like he owned my body. He would push me around, call me names, then take me to bed. He made me feel like it was my duty to 'perform.' "

When Lonny was sober, he wouldn't remember the things he'd done to hurt Rosalyn. "I'm sorry, Babe, I'm really sorry," he said over and over. But the scenes were just replayed another day.

"The fear and coldness within grew and grew," she says. "It was like being shut in a cold, dark cellar, and no one was with me to feel what I was feeling. Lonny was all I had, and I didn't really have him."

Thinking back to this time Lonny says, "When I hear other people tell about their marriages beginning to go bad, their stories are filled with all kinds of emotions and feelings. But at that point in my life, my story seems to be an absence of any emotions and feelings."

In her helplessness to "fix" things, Rosalyn found herself crying out for help. At one point she tried to leave him . . . and ended up accidentally running over Lonny with the car when he chased her. ("My friends started calling me 'retread,' " Lonny jokes. "It seems funny now, but it sure wasn't then.") Even though Lonny didn't press charges, Rosalyn still ended up feeling like things were always her fault, and her resentment seethed.

"Once I took an overdose to get rid of the chaos," she recalls, "but at the hospital they saved me. When I came to I wondered, *Is this my punishment for marrying an alcoholic when everyone told me not to?*"

Another time Rosalyn started to file for divorce, but never followed through. Cari was now entering her teen years, and Luke was a strapping 10 year old. Nothing had changed. She started to sink into a depression.

"Lonny just kept drinking and passing out," Rosalyn says. "I was so lonely I committed adultery twice with his best friend. I didn't tell Lonny for about five years. I just kept the guilt inside all that time, thinking I was punishing myself for what I had done as a little girl, for all the times I had sexual relationships with boys, for not being a good girl."

Love is an action. Like playing catch, love is generated in the active exchange of thoughts, words, and deeds which keep the feelings of love alive. When a relationship breaks down it is only natural that the loving feelings fade. This experience affects all marriages.

But the goals of marriage go far beyond "feeling in love" all of the time. Confirming the foundational commitment to the marriage helps ride out the lonely times.

At this point in Rosalyn and Lonny's lives they were running on "automatic pilot." Their responses to each other were determined by the tendencies in their personalities, survival strategies they saw modeled in their childhood, and basic fight-or-flight instincts.

As in many marriages, the cycles of dysfunction play out: One spouse's demand is countered by the other one's withdrawal; conflict is followed by self-protection; loneliness leads to isolation . . . anger . . . drink.

What Rosalyn and Lonny didn't know is that how we handle discomfort and pain is one of the most important aspects of our lives.

Lonny had been through a couple of jobs since he'd been laid off from the Chrysler plant, with no job at all for a year and a half. Rosalyn's job at a clothing factory wasn't enough to keep up with the bills, so just before Christmas of Cari's twelfth year, the Hansens had to file for bankruptcy.

It was a terrible blow. It meant losing the farm they'd hung on to for over seven years as well as Lonnie's pride and joy — a

'79 pickup truck. "Everything we've worked for, Rosalyn," he groaned. Rosalyn realized that Lonny was shaken to the core; it made him start thinking about things.

The family moved off the farm and rented a house in town. But the drinking didn't stop and Rosalyn's depression worsened. Their life seemed like it was slowly being sucked down a bottomless hole. Desperate, she went for counseling at a nearby psychiatric center.

Unknown to Lonny, she also began attending an Al-Anon support group for spouses of alcoholics. It was like one last gasp for help. The acknowledgement of a Higher Power in the group made her hungry for more spiritual input and she started to go to church — something she hadn't done since she was a small child. (They hadn't even had a church wedding because her father just wanted to get it over with.)

A year after the bankruptcy, when it felt like they'd reached the lowest point ever, she somehow summoned the strength to give Lonny an ultimatum:

"Lonny, I've filed for a divorce."

He acted indifferent. "What about it? You don't really want to leave me and the kids."

"No, I don't. That's why I wrote into the

divorce papers that if you will agree to go to an alcohol treatment center to get some help, I'll drop the proceedings." Rosalyn took a deep breath. "But otherwise, it's final."

Lonny stared at her. Rosalyn met his gaze steadily. She was sure now; she couldn't go on. It was now . . . or never.

Lonny finally broke the silence. "Yeah, I know I've got a problem," he said somberly. "Okay, I'll do it."

Rosalyn could hardly believe her ears. "You'll do it? You'll get help?"

"Yeah. Where do I start?"

For starters, Lonny began attending AA (Alcoholics Anonymous) meetings. He also agreed to go for counseling at the same psychiatric center.

But Rosalyn was in shock. "I had real mixed emotions when Lonny finally admitted that he had a problem and began to go for help," she admits. "It was hard to even think about reconciliation, because it seemed I had lost all love for him. I knew I had once really loved him, and that he had loved me. But so much of the feeling was gone that I found it hard to believe we could love each other again.

"I had anxiety attacks — real panic — even when things were going relatively well, and I wasn't sure where the fear was coming from. Gradually, my counselor helped me see that my fear of being hurt again if the drinking should start over was very deep.

"But," she continues, "when I finally had some breathing room, I began to see that the reason I had never followed through with divorce proceedings was that something deep inside told me divorce was against my will as a responsible adult. For the first time I felt real hope."

As for Lonny, at the AA meetings he found people who understood and cared. It was the first step on the long road to understanding his addiction and recovering from it. "At first," he admits, "I felt like a little lost boy with nowhere to go. I was scared and afraid I couldn't handle this new outlook on life.

"But my first real feeling of hope was when I finally admitted to myself that I was an alcoholic. I had been denying it for so long, I couldn't see the things I was doing. My mind always twisted things around so that when bad things happened, they were always other people's fault. Now I knew that I needed help. I also knew that it was all right to get help. I wasn't an evil person; I had an addiction that people could help me learn to control."

One thing Lonny discovered was that he

didn't have to take a drink. And that meant no more blackouts where he couldn't remember what happened; no more fighting like cats and dogs with Rosalyn; no more hangovers.

But Lonny also knew there was always a chance of relapsing. "I could let it happen; it was totally up to me," he realized. "I knew I would need lots of help, but I also knew I could do it."

A second step Lonny took was to join a co-dependency group for a week of treatment at the psychiatric center. "Several of us spent the time learning how to express feelings we had always stuffed down inside before." To Lonny, learning how to express his anger in healthy ways and how to let things go was like a huge sigh of relief.

Rosalyn had thrown down the gauntlet and made the challenge; Lonny had accepted the challenge, and now they had started on the road to recovery. As Rosalyn says, "It felt like someone had taken that beer bottle and shattered it into tiny pieces. Now we could work on other things in our marriage without Lonny's drinking always coming between us."

One issue Rosalyn had to face was being depressed so much of the time. "I kept feeling this was because I was a bad person, or because Lonny was a bad person. But with counseling I discovered that my depression is an illness, and that it can be treated like an illness once we understand where it is coming from."

Unfortunately, their families on both sides didn't understand what Lonny and Rosalyn were doing — and still don't. "I wish they did," says Rosalyn wistfully, "because their support would be a big help. They can't understand us being willing to spend what it has cost to get help. They say, 'You just need to grow up and face your responsibilities.' But they never knew what went on behind closed doors. And they don't realize how much richer their own lives could be if they would get some help. The help we've received has made our lives so much more worth living."

"I need help."

"I have a problem I want to change."

"I'm not able to continue like this."

These words are the beginning of a new relationship. When a spouse admits weakness and vulnerability, the need for self-protection is ended. Without the walls of self-protection, open and honest communication can finally take place.

When Rosalyn and Lonny both came to the place of acknowledging that they couldn't lick their problems alone, intimacy had a chance.

A healthy relationship relies on a growing self-awareness of each spouse and the ability not only to share (give) insights growing out of this awareness, but to hear (receive) the insights of the other.

Roadblocks to healthy living and relating must be conquered. Note the internal and external resistance to change. Also note all the resources Lonny and Rosalyn used to overcome this resistance!

The gut-level honesty of AA meetings helped Lonny begin to get to know himself — which wasn't always easy. "When all the issues I needed to face looked like too much for me, I learned to be content to grow one day at a time," he says. "Rosalyn was going through her own therapy for depression. I couldn't understand what she was going through, but I was able to suffer along with her. Because I was sober, I started to get in touch with her feelings, as well as with my own. We actually started to grow in our understanding and communication with each other. And that's how we began to love each other all over again."

Life is a lot different now for the Hansens, but they would be the first ones to admit that it didn't happen overnight. "I'm learning that recovery is a lifetime process," says Rosalyn. "You don't just get things fixed and never have to worry about them again. We will always have struggles, but the hard work of facing our problems has been worth every moment."

Besides the counseling they've done both alone and together at the psychiatric center, Rosalyn also took a week of the co-dependency program. "That program helped me work with others in discovering how the things I do affect Lonny and other people, and also how to begin changing what needs to be changed."

Rosalyn's continuing membership in Al-Anon has also given her a circle of friends who help her learn to control her anger, frustration, self-pity, and depression.

As for her church involvement, she says, "Church activities are more important to me than I ever thought they could be. I am a Sunday school teacher now, and a deaconess in my church. The church has also helped us do some financial planning as a family and to get on a workable budget."

"Through all of these things," she admits, "I am learning to live my own life, so that everything I do isn't just a reaction to Lonny. At the same time I am learning how to communicate my feelings, needs, and wants to him. I'm learning to listen to his feelings and needs and wants. Even though I am learning to live my life, I want to share it with my husband and children. I had never known that was possible! But I feel like God has untied all those knots in my heart and filled it full of love, flowing in and out freely. It's so beautiful to feel warmth and compassion toward other people."

Slowly, Lonny and Rosalyn are learning practical ways to keep their relationship growing. For instance, they set aside time for listening to one another, even if it's only a half-hour each day. They have also been getting away for a weekend every few months — "with no kids, no dog, no phone calls — just the two of us."

"We listen to the old love songs we used to listen to when we were dating," Rosalyn grins. "We take walks and hold hands. It's our time to say, 'I love you; I need you.' "

"On one of our weekends away we went to a magic show with David Copperfield," Lonny remembers. "We stayed in a motel near the performance hall, and it was heaven. We shared some intimate moments together, and it meant so much to spend the whole weekend with someone I really love and care about. Now I'm learning to do magic tricks and I'm pleased that Rosalyn can enjoy being part of something I enjoy."

Lonny and Rosalyn are learning the value of making time for each other with no interruptions. "I'm learning that if I can accept my wife just as she is, then I can also begin to be myself," says Lonny. "For me, it takes these weekends away with no worry about the kids or the dog or anything else. We know we have to sacrifice some other things to make that possible every few months, but our relationship is worth it."

Another important growing edge has been learning how to become interested in what the other is doing. "For instance, I started going to church with Rosalyn," says Lonny, "and this has made her very happy, because her church has become a big part of her life. Now this is another interest we share together."

Just when the Hansens start thinking they have it all together, however, something happens. "But we're also discovering a strength we didn't know we had," Rosalyn maintains. "And we're willing to give it all we've got. I know for a fact that Lonny and I could never have recovered to this point on our own. We have to keep learning to communicate, and to do that we've really needed that third person (our counselor) to be a kind of interpreter."

Lonny agrees. "I'm sure we will need our marriage counselor for some time yet. At one time I might have thought we couldn't afford it, but now I know that our marriage is priceless and worth anything we have to put into it."

I believe there is a "Plan A" for everyone — formed by God, blessed by Christ, empowered by the Holy Spirit. Obstacles to "Plan A" require attention. Most couples in despair wonder if they have the strength to make the changes. Yes, healthy relationships take patience and persistence. But sick living is taxing, too. In time, maintaining a good marriage is less stressful than the old, destructive ways. Besides, abundant living is rewarding, while efforts to maintain a broken life only drain the human spirit.

Lonny sums up the struggle they've been through this way: "It's like I had been strapped in a straitjacket for years, struggling and trying to escape. But I'm not a good enough magician to get out of a straitjacket by myself. Others had to help me out. But once I escaped from it, the pressure is off. And now that I am not bound, I can choose what I want. I am choosing love and happiness."

As for the effect on their children, who

were 11 and 16 at the time Rosalyn delivered her "ultimatum," she says, "Even though we've had to be away from our children some to work at our counseling and to have time for just ourselves, Cari and Luke have received so much love and warmth which had previously been absent, I feel they have gained rather than suffered. The way things were before, it was always hard to talk to them without screaming."

Both Lonny and Rosalyn agree that as their marriage gets more healthy, so does their family life. "It is so different for the kids than it might have been," Rosalyn reflects. "If Lonny and I had given up on each other, they would be getting less than one-half of a family. They could only relate to us one at a time, not sharing at all in that third dimension, the warm relationship we now have between us."

Rosalyn says it's a wonderful feeling to tell their children together that they love them, and give them a leisurely kiss before they go to bed. Then she adds, "I wonder how different my life would have been if I had been told that as a child?"

Chapter Two

Sick and Tired of Being Sick and Tired

Matt Bentley heard the car pull into the driveway, the slam of a door, and a moment later his wife's key in the lock. He met her in the front hallway.

"Hilary, where have you been?" he demanded, his worry taking on a sharp tone now that she was home safe.

"Oh! Uh — I just went over to see Betsy for a while," Hilary said lightly, shrugging off her jacket and hanging it in the hall closet. "Did you pick up the dry cleaning like I asked?"

He knew the tactic well. Change the subject. Catch your spouse off guard. Shift the focus to the other person.

Why had he forgotten the dry cleaning? But he heard himself saying, "Oh, yeah, sure."

"Well, where is it?"

He was irritated. He wanted to shift the

focus back to her unexplained absence. But he'd lost the high ground now, and he knew it.

"Uh, probably in the car."

"Okay. I'll go get it."

"No, wait. I'll get it."

But she was already out the door to his car. When she came back in with no dry cleaning, she just looked at him with annoyance.

"Well, I was going to pick it up," he said lamely.

Hilary's pretty face, framed by her wire-rimmed glasses and shagged hair, clouded over with unspoken anger. "Guess I'll have to pick it up myself."

"You didn't leave a note," Matt said lamely, trying to recapture the conversation. But he knew it was useless.

Hilary ignored his comment and headed for the kitchen. "I hate wearing a dress in the bookstore. . . ." Her voice faded and he heard cupboard doors opening, then it reappeared again. ". . . but your mom wants me to wear something 'presentable' when I wait on customers." Bang went a pot.

Still standing in the front hall, Matt sighed. She was lying about going to see Betsy. He knew it because . . . because it was the same kind of deceit he practiced with her every day.

"Going to take out the trash, Hon." (Just an excuse, any excuse, to tuck away a couple beers in the garage.)

"Could I have seconds?" (Holding up his wine glass with a benign smile as she willingly gave him a refill — knowing she was unaware of the two refills he'd already had when she left the room, first to get the main dish out of the oven and then to answer the phone.)

Always paying cash at the liquor store so she wouldn't know how much booze he bought . . . stashing the empties in the garage and taking them out himself on trash days so she didn't see all the bottles . . . doing most of his drinking when she wasn't around . . . giving vague answers after he'd stopped at a bar for a few quick ones.

And today. He knew why he forgot to pick up the dry cleaning. He wanted to get home fast, because he really needed a drink.

Matt caught a glimpse of himself in the front hall mirror: round, pleasant face; a high forehead making inroads into his brown curly hair; glasses sitting on his fine-featured nose. A mouth that could curve into a charming grin.

He winced. What he really saw was an alcoholic putting on a front.

A great sadness washed over him and he squeezed his eyes shut to block out his image. It was one thing to lie himself; as long as Hilary and others didn't know how much he drank, he could fool himself into thinking it wasn't that bad. But he looked up to Hilary to be the strong one; he counted on Hilary. If Hilary was lying to him . . . he knew it was only a matter of time until his whole world came apart.

• • •

Hilary's heart was pounding as she jerked cupboards open and noisily pulled a cast iron skillet out from under the jumble of pans. What was Matt doing home? She thought he would be working late ordering stock at the bookstore. She meant to get home before he did . . . but now what was going to happen? Did he suspect? Did he realize his wife and his mother were gone from the family bookstore at the same time? Did he put two and two together and figure out his family was "plotting" to confront him?

Suddenly Hilary felt like she was going to cry. She dashed into the bathroom, locked the door, and held a towel over her mouth to stifle the sobs that came wrenching to the surface. She had only recently worked up the courage to do an intervention — the whole family confronting the alcoholic to help break into the denial. It was her one last hope to save her marriage. But if Matt discovered the plan . . . no! It had to work! She couldn't bear to just go on and on, seeing her husband hide behind his drink and denials, shutting himself in, shutting her out.

They were only going through the motions as a married couple. Matt often waited to come to bed until he thought she was asleep, then lay with his back toward her. He didn't get angry, he didn't yell . . . he just wasn't there. He seemed lost inside himself. It didn't seem to matter whether she was there or not. Even without words, the rejection cut deep.

It hadn't always been this way. Hilary thought back eight years to when she first met Matt Bentley. She had been almost 29, working for the Red Cross in Washington, DC, and wondering if she would be single the rest of her life. On a trip home to North Carolina, a friend introduced her to a man in the city parks department who attended the same church as Hilary's parents. Matt Bentley was 35 (six years older than she) and divorced, with two children who lived with his ex-wife.

Hilary had been single a long time. She had dated a lot of guys but had never met anyone she felt right about before now. Almost from the first time she went out with Matt, she didn't feel single anymore.

Matt and Hilary were married six months later. Hilary reports, "I felt so happy and peaceful and sure. Even when Matt lost his city job four months later, it was still okay. We knelt and prayed in our little apartment, and kept on going. Between my piano students and his unemployment stipend, we barely scraped by. He seemed depressed and drank quite a bit, but he never got violent or angry — just quiet. So I kept excusing him, mostly because I had had hard times too, and other people were patient with me."

Hilary knew about hard times. Being a child of the sixties and seventies, she'd been a self-styled hippie during some of those years, and fairly promiscuous. At age 20 she got pregnant, and gave birth to a baby boy. Her parents were mortified and tried to keep the whole thing secret. Knowing she didn't have her act together and couldn't provide a real home for a child, she agreed to give up the baby for adoption.

"It'll be all right," a friend assured her during one of her crying spells after giving the baby up. "You'll have other children later on, when you're married and ready to settle down. And you'll know you did the best thing for this one." It was the same advice she'd heard from her parents, her lawyer, her social worker, and the maternity nurse.

But it didn't feel all right. The confusion and denied pain fed the craziness of the hippie years. Then, in her mid-twenties, someone introduced her to Jesus. Her spiritual conversion brought peace and stability into Hilary's life. She also felt a new longing to be married. Still some time passed before she met Matt.

After all those years of wondering if she'd ever have more children, she stood with Matt at the church altar, smiled into his beaming face, and said, "I do." There was no need to dwell on the past now; the future was ahead. After all, Matt loved kids, and together they looked forward to having children. But they didn't rush it; good thing, since Matt lost his job just a few months later. Hilary wasn't worried; after all, he had fathered two children already, and she was still young. They had time.

Everyone has an inner world of thoughts and feelings. Sometimes we're aware of our private side, sometimes we're not. No person has a total grasp of what's going on inside. And no marriage is so intimate as to have a total understanding of each other.

We should seek self-awareness and mutual understanding in our marriage, but this is only partially attainable. Knowing every moment of another person's life is not essential. However, our inner world, whether private or secret, will be reflected in our public lives and actions.

A private world is different from a secret world. Being by oneself is different from hiding. Unfortunately Matt and Hilary are in hiding — both from themselves and from each other.

But the outward signs and symptoms still abound. Hilary may not have a daily blood-alcohol reading on her husband, but she's aware of the consequences. Hilary's inner pain may go verbally uncommunicated, but in time generates her angry responses.

When the Bentleys did decide to try for a child, months went by and Hilary did not get pregnant. Somewhat anxious, she suggested they both get medical checkups; Matt agreed. Hilary made an appointment with her gynecologist and began fertility workups.

"Did you make a doctor's appointment yet?" Hilary asked her husband.

"Oh! Hil! I forgot," Matt said, slapping the side of his head contritely. "I'll call tomorrow."

After a few workups, Hilary's initial fertility tests showed nothing amiss. "The next tests involve surgical procedures," her gynecologist explained. "Before we go that direction, however, we should know the results of your husband's tests." So Hilary asked Matt a second time if he'd made an appointment.

"Yeah, yeah, I took care of it and everything's fine," he assured her. But she never saw any paperwork.

Doesn't Matt know how important this is to me? Hilary fumed. Not just me — us! I thought we both wanted children. Frustrated, she called Matt's doctor and discovered what she already suspected: Matt had not been tested at all. She set up an appointment and went with him to be sure. When the test results came back, the doctor talked to them together.

"I'm afraid your diabetes has made you sterile, Matt," said the doctor. "It's one of the possible side effects of the disease, and at your age. . . ."

Both Matt and Hilary were stunned. On the way home, Matt said, "I'm sorry, Honey. I-I had no idea."

"It's not your fault," said Hilary in a small voice. "We just have to accept it and say 'Praise the Lord' anyway."

She said the words, but at home grief and disappointment gave way to tears —

floods and floods of tears.

Miserably, Matt retreated with another drink. Familiar feelings of failure seemed to sap all the strength out of him. First, his divorce after 11 years of marriage; then losing his job with the city. Months of unemployment were becoming years, and still no solid leads. And now this.

Matt tried to shake off the uneasy feelings. "No big deal," he told himself. After all, he did have two children from his first marriage even though he didn't get to see them. And he was pushing 40; maybe he was too old to be thinking about babies, anyway. Still . . . he knew Hilary was devastated. But, what could he do about it?

Unable to handle Hilary's tears, Matt withdrew a little further into his shell and did what he could to bury the pain deeper.

Hilary, meanwhile, tried to push down the anger she felt. After all, she tried to rationalize, Matt can't help it. That's just the way it is. But why did he keep "forgetting" to make an appointment? Did he suspect the diabetes? Was he hoping her tests would turn up something so it would be her fault?

One Saturday while Matt was out doing a temporary job, the anger boiled out and she spent the whole day yelling at God. "This is such a mean trick!" she screamed in the empty house. "I was single for so long, and I'd already given up my only child! Then You gave me a husband who already had two children. I thought that was Your assurance to me that he was going to give me children, too! You let me down!"

It wasn't fair!

Finally her rage was spent. But disappointment and a dull grief took up residence in her spirit which would last for several years.

Meanwhile, Matt's little deceptions to hide the extent of his drinking became an unconscious habit. Looking back now, he says, "My interest in sex diminished and my ability to show affection slipped away. How could I get close to Hilary when she would smell that I had been drinking? No one could drink that much and not reek of booze! The only time I felt safe in getting close to her was when she would drink, too — which wasn't very often. But at those times she drank enough to lose all interest in me." He was caught in a vicious trap, but had no energy or strength to do anything about it. "I needed so much to be loved," Matt says, "but I had lost the ability to express love to my spouse, or to anyone else."

At that time, Hilary didn't understand alcohol and didn't make a fuss about Matt's drinking. "I didn't even know about most of it," she admits. "All I knew is that he just seemed to withdraw from me. It really hurt to be ignored. I thought, *If Matt doesn't love me or want me, then probably nobody would.*"

Our interpretations of what things mean directly influences how we feel. Without open, clarifying communication, couples get caught in a pattern of reacting to misinterpretations.

Each partner — hurting, hungry, hopeless — turns away. The person we expected the most from is letting us down. These are the powerful feelings of despair.

The Bentleys had only been married three years, appearing to their friends as a happy couple. But, as Hilary recalls, "I felt like there were rats eating away at the fabric of our lives. I couldn't see them or identify them, so I didn't know what to do. Matt would tell me everything was fine, and I wanted to believe him. But things didn't feel fine to me. I felt so confused and depressed, and didn't even know why."

One particularly bad day, Hilary couldn't seem to stop crying. Even though she had told herself she would never do this, she packed a bag, left Matt a dramatic note, and called her parents to come get her. "I felt so awful," she remembers. "I was miserable, disappointed, frightened, and lonely. All my hope for our marriage was gone. All evening at my folks' house I cried and waited for Matt to call . . . but he never did."

When Matt found Hilary's note, it seemed like a yawning chasm had opened up in front of him. He really loved Hilary and didn't want to lose her! What was he going to do? He had to think! Packing some camping gear in the car, Matt drove up into the nearby mountains and spent the night in much the same state as his wife: "miserable, frightened, and lonely."

The next day he called Hilary. She came home and they talked. She tried to tell him how rejected she felt; she didn't understand why he was shutting her out of his life. Not being able to have a child was still painful — but it was more than that.

"Hilary," Matt said, taking a deep breath, "I need to tell you something — something I should have told you before we got married. I-I have a drinking problem. And I think that's the reason our marriage is in trouble."

Hilary's first reaction was shock — Matt? an alcoholic? — then embarrassment (What will my friends think!) "But I felt relieved, too," says Hilary. "The trouble we were having had a name to put on it." In a flurry of good intentions, they attended some AA and AlAnon meetings, and Hilary read a few books on the subject. But attendance at the meetings soon dropped off. Within a few months the old patterns had reappeared, and life settled back into dreariness and pain.

But at least now Hilary knew the name of the enemy. After his night on the mountain, Matt had said so clearly, "Alcoholism has eaten away at our life, at our strength, and our hope." That was true. Hilary had been patient for so long that she felt half dead. "I couldn't figure out another thing to do to make it okay," she says now, "so I just gave up. I told God if He wanted me to live in a rented apartment with an alcoholic for the rest of my life, it was His business. But I was very disappointed . . . and mad at God, too."

About that time, while away at a professional conference, Hilary gave in to an old habit pattern and had a brief affair with another man. "I was so tired of feeling rejected and shut out of Matt's life," she says. "It was a relief to know someone might want me. Yet that affair scared me so much that within a year I had sex with someone else — another one-night stand — to break the uniqueness of the first. I hated myself for falling back into old patterns and struggled quite a while before God helped me to get free. I really did desire to be faithful to God and His principles, and that kept me going in spite of everything."

As for Matt, he saw his marriage crumbling, but he, too, felt helpless to do anything about it. "I married Hilary because I loved her very much," he reflects. "My first wife and I had eloped as teens when she got pregnant. It was difficult from the start and ended in a painful divorce.

"In contrast, Hilary was almost everything I wanted in a wife, and we were no longer kids. I knew this marriage would be different; our families were supportive and we had a ceremony in the church. I thought I'd gone into this marriage wide awake, and that with enough love and God's blessing I could not fail — again — as a husband."

But he could fail. Matt was a practicing alcoholic when he married Hilary, though unwilling to admit it until that day when she left him and went home to her parents. "At that point," he says, "my self-esteem and ability to function productively, which had never been very high, reached a real low point. I was overwhelmed with guilt, loneliness, fear, shame, and the overpowering sense of failure. I kept hearing inside my head, 'You can't do anything right' — an expression I had often heard as a child."

Matt had grown up as the "lost child" in an alcoholic family. His father's addiction to drink controlled the family; his mother functioned as an "enabler," manipulating his father in her efforts to hold things together. Matt's younger brother was the capable "hero," who created a measuring stick by which Matt was compared.

"Don't make any trouble," his mother told him constantly. "Be home right after school. Why can't you be more like your brother?" He learned the lesson of hiding the truth well.

After confessing his "drinking problem" to Hilary, Matt continued to drink. "I no longer had the energy to keep up the phony front. My life centered around alcohol," he admits now. "I was drinking 24 hours a day and telling myself that I would quit tomorrow — trying to hold on to the barest hope by telling myself it wasn't that bad yet."

Not only does drinking affect a person's relationships, but it affects the body as well. Addictions are strong, compulsive cravings. Physically and emotionally the alcoholic has the sensation of being "off-balance," "unable to cope," "in trouble" without alcohol.

It is almost as though a distorted mental

and physical belief sets in. Alcohol is viewed as a natural bodily chemical. The alcoholic experiences a constant "alcohol deficiency." But an alcoholic drinking alcohol is like a thirsty man drinking salt water. Momentarily there is relief, but in the long run the relief turns out to be poison.

That same year, however, after several months of outright unemployment, Matt got a job helping his mother open a bookstore. Hilary told herself that now things would be better. "When I was asked to join the family business, I was glad to help make it work. I ended up staying for four years because I became indispensable."

Even though "getting a job" should have relieved some of the financial stress the Bentleys were experiencing, it didn't turn out that way. "Oh, there were some good things about it," Hilary acknowledges. "Books and customers are fine. But the financial aspect was horrible. Bentley Books didn't have enough capital to run properly, and yet we needed to get a living out of it."

Hilary did what she could to get the finances under control, "But Matt and my mother-in-law ran the day-to-day aspects," she says wryly. "This created a tremendous amount of conflict."

Matt, too, shakes his head over this state

of affairs. "I had been unable to manage our financial affairs in any semblance of order ever since we got married," he admits. "If anything got paid by me it was an accident. The only thing I was interested in financially was enough money for booze. When the bookstore thing opened up, Hilary and I were supposedly working together in a family business, but in reality, she spent a great deal of time and energy covering for me or rescuing me. All of these things added to the burden of guilt I heaped on myself and further lowered my self-esteem."

According to Hilary, "I never got paid; I just caught the brunt of the emotional stress. We usually managed to get enough money out of the bookstore to cover the rent, but not much more. I guess Matt took out quite a bit of money for alcohol and pornographic magazines — which left me feeling both helpless and angry. I resented not having enough money for things I needed. My mother bought me shoes and clothes when I had to have them. I coped by crying a lot and sleeping a lot."

Not long after Matt and Hilary began working at the bookstore, they got a phone call from his ex-wife. "Your daughter wants to come live with you," the voice on the phone said matter-of-factly. "Do you have any room for her?" Both Matt and Hilary said yes. Cheri arrived a week later, a scared and rebellious 17 year old.

("We found out later," says Hilary, "that her mother had given her a choice between seeing a psychiatrist once a week, being placed in a foster home, or going to live with her dad!") When Cheri moved out on her own a year later, Matt's 16-year-old son Jamie moved in. Life became even more complicated.

Many times Hilary has wondered what kept them going during those years. "I thought I should be able to live through our situation without any fuss or trouble. I was convinced God meant us to be together and so this must be my cross to bear. After all, other people had it worse, didn't they?

"Also," she adds, "although there was a lot of pain with Matt, we did have some special times and tender moments that kept us hanging on. Bittersweet, I guess. So I just kept trying and hoping."

Strangely, one of the hardest things Matt faced during this time was the silence. "Nobody — not Hilary, not my family, not my church — confronted me about my drinking during those last few years. It seemed like nobody cared enough to challenge me about my slow death, the death of our relationship and marriage, my deteriorating health, my inability to communicate.

"I was losing almost everything I had once cared about. I lost most of my ability to function as a husband and lover, all interest in recreation, all interest in church or God's saving grace, all interest in social functions and family gatherings — just about everything except getting the garbage out to the curb each week, and that was only because I needed more room to dispose of empty bottles."

Rock bottom.

No place to go but up.

We all have a threshold for what we determine to be the end of the line. Some people tolerate a lot before they go to work at recovery. Others only tolerate and exist.

While there is always plenty of hindsight, the reality seems to be that we are complicated creatures of timing. Predicting what it takes for a person to begin changing is like trying to predict the weather — especially when alcohol is involved.

For Matt and Hilary, it seemed like they'd hit bottom, but the issues and the relationship were muddy. They had not yet hit hard, cold reality.

Hilary took a trip to Houston to visit an

old college roommate, "just to get away." On Sunday, her friend took her to an Episcopal renewal parish to worship. As Hilary recalls it, "The first thing I noticed was that the whole congregation was saying the Lord's Prayer together real loud as if they all meant it! It's unusual in an Episcopal parish for people to raise their voices.

"Then during community prayers, the priest said, 'Let's pray for Dennis and Rita Bennett as they begin the healing conference here this week.' My mouth fell open. I had gotten a notice for that conference several weeks ago and had just thrown it away, because there was just no way I could go. Now it was like Jesus had sent an invitation to me on a silver platter: 'My daughter, would you like to go?' Here I was, with nothing standing in the way between me and that conference."

The healing conference was a spiritual turning point for Hilary. "I received a 'healing of memory' having to do with various rejections I'd experienced during my life. I didn't fully understand it, but there was a definite healing." A second significant event was a word from a fellow conference attender, who had no idea what Hilary's personal situation was: "If a person is on a chemical substance, almost always they must first be removed from the substance before the prayers can get through."

Then Hilary knew what she had to do. The combination of these two events gave her the courage and determination to begin planning an "intervention" on Matt's behalf — when all family members agree that their loved one needs help, and work together to see that it happens.

Once back home in North Carolina, unknown to Matt, she called a meeting with Matt's two children, his mother, his brother, and her parents. "That meeting actually helped us to know as a family that Matt was an alcoholic," says Hilary. "Before, each person only knew a little piece, but when we shared our own experience and observations, then we could see the big picture."

It was after that meeting that Matt confronted Hilary in the front hall, wanting to know where she'd been. Her bold-faced lies scared him. Why was she being so deceptive? "It didn't take me long to figure out what was going on," he says. "Part of me was ready to go into alcohol treatment. But I had to be in control. Without letting on that I suspected what was up, I began to do my own thing to cause interruptions and try to control the situation."

About this time, Matt's son Jamie

wrecked their pickup when he should have been in school, and the police found a case of beer in the cab. Ironically, Matt wanted to talk about getting him into treatment!

This was almost too much for Hilary. Here she was, working with the son to intervene in his father's life, and working with her husband to intervene in his son's!

Then, the morning of the critical intervention, Matt's mother called Hilary and bowed out.

"But Mom Bentley! Why? I thought we agreed that Matt needs help, and he isn't about to check into the hospital by himself!" Hilary tried not to sound desperate.

"But that's so drastic," said her mother-in-law cautiously. "For instance, maybe he would listen to me if I talked to him. I haven't even tried asking him to stop drinking."

"Oh, Mom," moaned Hilary. "That won't —"

"Well, I don't think his drinking is bad enough to hospitalize him. He's not the town drunk, you know. And I'm not going to be party to sneaking around behind his back."

Then Matt's brother called. "Sorry, Hilary," he said. "But if Mom's not on board with this intervention thing, it's not going to work. So count me out, too."

Discouraged, Hilary called her parents.

"I guess I'm going to have to cancel the meeting," she moaned. "Matt's family is bailing out, so you might as well not come either."

It looked like an "intervention" was not going to work. Frustrated and angry, Hilary realized she shouldn't have been surprised. Several generations of alcoholism in Matt's family had created a tangle of emotional binds and "co-dependence."

But this was her life and her marriage! She couldn't give up now. Even if she had to do the intervention all by herself, she had to try.

She called the treatment center at the hospital and talked to the counselor. The counselor said, "I'll be here all afternoon, Hilary. But you can't bring your husband in here unless you tell him the truth about what he's coming for."

Fear gripped Hilary. She had no guarantees that Matt would go into treatment. What if he leaves me? she thought, fighting back the panic that threatened to paralyze her. But no. They couldn't keep on like this. She had to take the risk.

"Matt," she said carefully, "remember that counselor we talked to about Jamie? I made an appointment with him for this afternoon. Would you go with me?"

Matt paused a moment, then nodded. "Okay."

Hilary was trembling as they pulled into the hospital parking lot. She had to tell him now.

"Matt," she said, swallowing hard, "this meeting isn't about Jamie's drinking. It's about you." With sheer willpower, Hilary quit staring out the windshield and looked at Matt. "Will you go with me anyway?"

Matt nodded. "Yes, I will."

Hilary blinked. Did he really understand what she meant? But as they sat in the counselor's office, the counselor spoke directly to Matt. "Matt, do you think you have a drinking problem?"

"Yes," said Matt.

"Do you think you're an alcoholic?"

"Yes."

"Would you come in for treatment?"

Again Matt said, "Yes."

"When do you want to come in?"

"How about tomorrow?"

Hilary was astonished. It was almost as if she'd asked, "Do you want to go to the movies tonight?"

"I knew it was the hand of God," she says, "because alcoholics don't willingly go into treatment very often. "

As for Matt, he says, "I was sick and tired

of being sick and tired."

The conversation most feared by both for so long was in fact the conversation of hope. A solution? No. A step of faith? Yes. We only need risk enough to take the step.

Often the message of well-meaning people is "don't get your hopes up." This advice seeks to protect us from wishing problems away or fantasizing a far-off future.

But hope is essential for life. Hope used correctly keeps us open to the possibilities of God's redemptive power. A healthy hope moves us through life one day at a time. Hilary's hope got Matt to the hospital parking lot. Matt's hope got him in the door.

True to his word, the next day Matt entered the hospital for treatment. "It was a very lonely and somewhat scary time for me," he says. "For the first time in my life I took an honest, in-depth look at my life, what I had become, and I found there was no one to blame for it but me." With the help of the hospital staff, Matt began to find out how being raised in an alcoholic home had affected him — especially how he had never dared to feel true feelings, nor was he allowed to express the feelings he did have. This was how the family coped, pretending that everything was okay. As Matt says now,

"Silence is not golden."

When Matt went into treatment, Hilary started going to AlAnon again. "I didn't think I needed it, but I went because spouses of alcoholics are supposed to go to AlAnon. After awhile I started to enjoy it. It was refreshing to be with other people who know exactly what you're saying when you only say a little bit."

At first the emphasis in the AlAnon program, "Focus on yourself," seemed rather selfish. Hilary gradually realized the Bible talked about the same paradox: "Love your neighbor in the same way and to the same extent as you love yourself." In other words, says Hilary, "I began learning that I owe myself some common respect and courtesy. When I take care of myself, then I can care genuinely for others. When I respect myself and tell myself the truth, then I can respect others."

Meanwhile, Matt was learning some of the same basic rules for a healthy self-concept and mutual respect for others. "Using the tools and resources I was learning in treatment, I began sharing my real feelings instead of saying what I thought others wanted to hear. I began to say things the way I saw and felt them — my own feelings. But it took practice. Who better to help that change take place than other recovering alcoholics who have gone through or are going through the same things? What an amazing discovery! I wasn't alone unless I chose to be."

When Matt came home from the hospital a month later, he began the process of reconciliation with Hilary and his family. "I started looking at our marriage and asking what I could do to make it work — because that's what I wanted to happen. However, I learned that no matter how much I might want someone else to change, I could only change me. What a great revelation and relief: I am only responsible for myself! I don't have to try to control other people's feelings, or be responsible for them. And I soon learned that taking care of myself is a full time job!" Besides the chemical dependency, Matt realized he'd been using alcohol to hide from reality.

For years Matt had lost interest in almost everything except the next drink. Now he began to read again: books, papers, magazines — anything related to the areas they were struggling with. Others in his support group did the same.

"I soon realized there is more information out there than any of us could possibly cover alone, so we'd each pass on things we'd read. A lot of the information is good, some not. I took what seemed useful and didn't dwell on the rest. But I see now that the more we know, the more options we have."

As for Hilary, "It was a good nine months after Matt got out of inpatient treatment before I started seeing that I might need some help for myself. When I began individual therapy, my counselor asked me to read a book about overcoming depression. I didn't know I was depressed until I read that book. It reminded me of the saying, 'Been down so long it looks like up to me.' "

About that same time Matt and Hilary also began marriage counseling. "I didn't think things were that bad," says Hilary, "but how bad do things have to get?"

Some of the old beliefs that need to change in the beginning of a recovery process are: this is the way life is; there's nothing I can do about it; life is hopeless.

During recovery these are replaced with: life is continually changing; I always have choices; life is a gift from God designed to be abundant.

Hilary and Matt stepped out of one context filled with old views, limited options, and inadequate coping skills and placed themselves in new contexts where new understandings and strategies might be found.

In counseling, Hilary had to face some things that, even now, she'd rather not talk about. "Because of my confusion over my pregnancy at age 20, I ended up looking for comfort in sexual relationships and became fairly promiscuous. It fit into the hippie culture during those years. But now I believe I was dealing with a sexual addiction.

"When I was 25 I became a Christian, and God gave me a lot of grace to be pure for quite a while. But after I married Matt, I thought his rejection meant that I was unlovable. In panic, I looked for comfort in sexual relationships which led to the two brief affairs. But that frightened me so much, it shut me down even more and was very damaging — not just to our marriage, but to my own self-esteem."

After those affairs, Hilary remained distressed for several years. She finally confessed to a pastor friend and he ministered forgiveness to her. "That was much better," says Hilary, "but the secret of it still hassled me." She knew that God had forgiven her . . . but she was still troubled by it. What was worse, the treatment center where Matt had been had a saying: "You're only as sick as the secrets you keep."

Hilary thought, *I've got a secret and I*

can't tell . . . what am I going to do? If I tell a single person, Matt might find out, and what would happen then?

But Hilary decided she didn't want to have a marriage with secrets, so she finally told Matt about the affairs. "It was horrible," she admits. "Telling the secret was agony for both of us. But it's so much better now. It was definitely better to bring the secrets out of the darkness and into the light."

Some people say you should never tell your spouse if you have an affair, but Hilary disagrees — provisionally. "I think it matters what kind of marriage you want to have. If I was still holding that secret," she says emphatically, "we couldn't be sharing our story today. There are other women like me out there, frightened to talk about things. It makes you feel so isolated. Secrets only lead to further addictive behavior, in food, sex, alcohol, drugs, spending, or something, to cover up the pain."

Learning about Hilary's affairs was very painful for Matt. "I know I'm not perfect myself, so I've had to work on my feelings concerning this area of our relationship. However, our relationship is not at risk — we are still building what I consider today a good, strong, and growing marriage."

There was another painful area that had

to be faced. "The pain of being childless was probably greater," Hilary says, "because of the son I had had, but gave away to adoption. There is something very deep and excruciating in not being able to raise your own child."

With Matt's support, she began a search for the son she had given up. To do so she had to face another family secret. "That's been very difficult," Hilary admits. "My parents were very embarrassed and ashamed. For example, my mom said, 'If I was a better mother, you wouldn't have gotten pregnant.' I thought that was interesting, since I was the one who was rebellious. She took so much responsibility."

Three years after the search began, Hilary was reunited with her son, who was by then 21 years old. When they met, he said, "I've never met anybody who was like me before!"

"He had been raised by people who were not part of his genetic pool," Hilary explained. "They didn't look like him, didn't talk like him, didn't act like him. Then he met me and I act like him, talk like him, look like him. He was blown away! I was, too. It was awesome to meet him; I handled it by thinking of him as a younger brother. There's a definite family resemblance and he's the same size my younger brother used to be at that age. But there were times when I couldn't even breathe. The astonishment of it all!"

The meeting uncovered many unresolved grief issues for Hilary, and it was helpful to get involved in a birth mothers support group. "A lot of healing has come through it all, not just for me, but for us as a couple as well," Hilary maintains.

How good do I want my relationship to be?

How much forgiveness and grace am I willing to give and receive?

What meaning and purpose in life do I seek?

What level of openness and intimacy prioritizes my life?

The answers to these types of questions fuel growth. Some only want the dirt swept under the rug and the mess shoved in the closet. Others go for a totally clean house.

Healing, abundance, wholeness, peace, truth, and freedom — these are the goals God has for us and our marriages.

At the writing of this story, Matt has been sober for eight years. He would be the first one to acknowledge the positive changes in his own life. "I've not only renewed my emotional health but my physical health as well. I established contact with a doctor who knows my medical history and will not play games with me."

One giant stride was wanting do things with Hilary again — "not because a husband is supposed to take his wife somewhere once in a while, but because I enjoy Hilary's company more than anyone else's!" Matt grins. "We enjoy picnics, fishing, movies, rides, walks, canoeing — because we've discovered that play is an important part of recovery and reconciliation."

With his new interest in life and love, Matt wanted to share that love with Hilary. "I began to think of ways to court her again, like dressing up and going to new places, going for walks in quiet places, sending her cards, even leaving notes that I've gone to the store and when I'll return. I'm trying to keep my commitments even in the little things, and it means a great deal, not only to my wife and loved ones, but to myself as well. This is how we've been able to build trust and recover our marriage." All of which has helped them rebuild a satisfying sexual relationship as well.

As Matt's respect for himself grew, his respect and understanding of others grew also. "This helped me develop a new faith in myself and my relationship with Hilary."

Hilary agrees. "Here's the deal," she says passionately. "We have recovered so much hope and life in our marriage that I am beginning to risk being myself. I'll tell you, it's scary! Maybe other people won't like me if they know what I'm really feeling and what I want and who I am. Maybe Matt won't like me if I'm not so agreeable all the time. Maybe I won't like myself. I think I will, though. At this point I'm ready and willing to grow and stretch."

Both Hilary and Matt believe their relationship can handle some honesty and genuineness. "We've been talking to each other more deeply and honestly," they say. "In the last few years, we have seen many positive changes in our life. Our commitment is stronger and on a more genuine basis. Now we're even doing more things apart and making our way as a couple through some uncharted territory."

Because of the growth in their marriage and in their individual self-confidence, both Hilary and Matt have left the family bookstore and are pursuing new careers through new training and job opportunities.

Both agree that marriage counseling was good for them, and they've been back a couple times since, whenever they've felt the need for clarification. But even though their marriage still has its ups and downs, today Matt grins and says, "I give us an A+!"

Chapter Three

Birthday or Beer?

Vic Miller came in the back door, hung up his hat and headed for the refrigerator. Boy! It sure was hot for September. That ice-cold beer was going to taste good.

"Hi, Dad."

Vic jumped. He hadn't even noticed Lucy, their teenage daughter, icing a cake on the kitchen table.

Lucy licked icing from her fingers and grinned at his blank face. "Mom's birthday, remember?"

"Oh . . . right! Nice cake," he nodded. He swung open the refrigerator door and reached for the beer. Only one can? Vic peered into the shelves. Milk . . . leftover meatloaf . . . half a loaf of bread . . . pickles . . . salad dressing . . . lemon juice . . . three odd plastic containers . . . but no more beer.

He was going to need more than one can! Maybe if he chucked a few in the freezer they'd get cold quick. He popped the top of the cold beer in his hand, took a long thirsty pull, then headed for the basement where he usually kept a case or two.

The box was empty.

This time Vic cussed right out loud.

Back in the kitchen, he grabbed his hat, found the checkbook, and headed back out to the driveway.

"Dad! Where are you going?" Lucy called to him from the screen door.

"Be back in a few minutes. Gotta pick up something at the store."

"Well, don't forget Mom's birthday. She'll be home at six. I'm making a nice supper —"

"Don't worry! I'll be back," he tossed over his shoulder as he climbed into the car. He finished off the can of beer and stashed the empty under the seat before turning the key. He didn't want to get stopped for having open alcohol in the car.

On the way to the liquor store, Vic suddenly realized he didn't have anything for Laura's birthday. Well, he could pick up something for her at the shopping center. Maybe some perfume . . . or something. With a funny feeling, he realized he didn't have a clue what Laura wanted for her birthday.

Vic frowned and tried to think as he pulled into the shopping center parking lot. They sure had been fighting a lot lately.

Maybe their age difference was showing up. It hadn't seemed to matter when they got married. He'd been 36; she, 24. They were both young, divorced, and determined to make it the second time around.

But . . . 10 years later, she was still in the prime of her youth and he was sliding fast toward 50! He took a quick glance in the car mirror — hair still dark brown, conservative glasses, neat moustache trimmed with gray — and sighed. No matter what he said or did, Laura seemed to find some fault with it.

A pickup pulled out of a parking space right by the liquor store and Vic turned the car into it. Before getting out he flipped open the checkbook to see how much he could spend, since he only had a dollar or two in cash on him. Wait a minute — there were several new entries that hadn't been deducted: Shoe Town . . . Lawn and Garden Center (was that where she got those daisy windmills flapping in the flower garden? — silliest things he ever saw) . . . Discount City. . . .

Vic mentally deducted each of the amounts to get a new balance. Twenty dollars! That was IT until payday? He couldn't get Laura a birthday present and a case of beer with 20 dollars!

Vic got out of the car and slammed the door. Well, it'd serve her right after spending so much money on stupid stuff they didn't need. Maybe this would teach her a lesson. She knew money was tight. He sure wasn't going to give up his case of beer just to buy her some perfume or other doodad — especially after she just spent a wad of money on twirling daisies and who-knows-what-all.

If she can spend money as she pleases, he thought, pulling open the liquor store door, *then I deserve to spend some money as I please. And what I want right now is that case of beer. The sooner I get it on ice, the better I'm gonna like it. Man, it's hot for September!*

• • •

Somehow the birthday card with "Love, Vic" scrawled at the bottom didn't make it. Laura was upset, and he knew it.

"Look," he said patiently after Lucy had cleaned away the cake plates and disappeared into her room to do homework, "I really wanted to get you a birthday present. But you spent so much money this week, there wasn't enough left in the checkbook! And we agreed not to use the credit cards except for gas and emergencies."

"There was enough for a case of

beer," she said stiffly.

"But, Laura, don't you see? If you hadn't spent so much money on . . . on those twirling daisies or whatever, there would have been plenty of money for both —"

"Oh, forget it!" Laura snapped. "All you care about is having enough beer. You leave the garden to me, the shopping to me; you never fix anything around this house so then I have to go out and replace it. But is that important? Am I important? Oh, no. Not as long as Vic Miller has a cold beer in his hand. Well, I don't care either. You can sit there and keep your beer company. I'm going in the kitchen to do the dishes!"

Vic watched his wife flounce into the kitchen and sighed. Now she was going to be a martyr — doing dishes on her birthday. But no way was he going to go in there and put up with her sarcasm. Why couldn't she see it? No money for a birthday present should have been a good object lesson: she had to cut down on her spending. Why did she keep dodging the obvious and keep harping about a few cans of beer?

Vic sighed, picked up the not-quite-cold can of beer from the table, wandered into the living room, and flicked on the TV.

• • •

In the kitchen, Laura Miller let the tears

of hurt and disappointment flow unhindered. She was only 34, but she felt as if she'd been married all her life . . . and she was so tired. She was only 17 when she got married the first time (*Just a few years older than Lucy!* she thought with a shock), a marriage that lasted all of six years, and the only good thing that came out of it was a beautiful daughter.

Now here she was in her second marriage, and just as miserable. Apparently she just couldn't be a good wife. Laura brushed a few stray curls out of her eyes with a sudsy hand, then slid the dirty plates into the dishwater. As a girl she had vowed never to marry a man who drank alcohol . . . so why did she?

After her divorce she had gone to work in a factory that manufactured parts for mobile homes, and Vic was her supervisor. She almost smiled through her tears, remembering. At 23, she'd been the first woman to ever work in that department, and he had gallantly stuck up for her. Vic was older and protective; she felt safe. She knew he drank, but he promised he would give it up if she married him. And he did . . . for a while. But now, he hardly seemed like the gentle, caring man she'd married.

Laura stacked the plates in a row in the

dish drainer and sprayed them with hot water. On the other hand, she admitted to herself, she wasn't the woman he had married, either. She knew he disliked the way she complained and criticized him. But she didn't like Vic much anymore, and . . . she didn't like herself much, either.

As with most couples whose marriage gets in trouble, the problems for Vic and Laura began many years earlier. A relationship doesn't change automatically from giving to taking . . . from vulnerability to self-protection . . . from tolerance to being demanding . . . from love to hate.

Marriages don't have good guys and bad guys forced together against their will. Marriages are made up of two people who willingly chose to become life partners. This union was full of hopes and dreams. So how can it get so bad?

Recalling her formative years, Laura says, "I never really had a childhood. My father was an alcoholic, and my parents divorced when I was eight years old. My dad moved 2,000 miles away to California, leaving my mom in Indiana with eight children. He never paid any child support, and she had to go to work to support us." The family was very poor; sometimes it seemed that all they had was each other. With all the responsibilities that fell to the kids, Laura just moved right into adulthood.

When she was 11 Laura started babysitting to earn money. One time the man for whom she was babysitting came home drunk and molested her. "I was so afraid of him after that, I wished he would die," she says. "I thought it must have been my fault somehow, and didn't tell my mother for fear she would blame me."

When Laura read the man's obituary years later, she felt as if an enormous weight had been lifted from her — then felt guilty for being glad he was dead. But at the time young Laura vowed she would never marry a man who drank.

"But I did," she says now. "I knew Vic had a problem with alcohol, but he promised me he wouldn't drink if I would marry him. I didn't think I could live without him and kidded myself that maybe my marrying him would help with his problem."

As for Vic, he was attracted to the pretty brunette with the winning smile in his department. Though there was 12 years difference in their ages, they enjoyed many of the same things, as well as just being with each other and their friends.

"Laura made it clear from the beginning

that she wanted nothing to do with an alcoholic," he concedes. "So I quit drinking and we began seeing each other regularly." Within a year they married — a second marriage for both. "But I just knew it was going to be better this time," says Vic.

"My first marriage ended because my wife and I were never able to agree on anything. Oh, yeah, I drank, but kept telling myself that had nothing to do with it. My father was an alcoholic and Mom raised us kids mostly by herself. I told myself I would never be an alcoholic because I could stop whenever I wanted to. But," he admits now, "after a few beers, I never wanted to."

Except . . . to marry Laura. And, she says, "We were really happy for a while. He got a different job, but I stayed on at the factory. We even took in three foster kids for a couple years. Then one by one his kids wanted to leave mama and come live with us — and the oldest boy was only six years younger than I was! I started blaming Vic for all the problems his ex-wife and kids were putting on us and thought I needed to help him take control of his life."

Even with the complication of step-children and ex-spouses, the marriage seemed pretty together for two and a half years. Then one afternoon the Millers were at a wedding reception. Vic thought, *Just one drink can't hurt anything.* But, he admits now, "After that one drink I was hooked again."

At first it was only a couple of beers in the evening, but then the drinking increased. Communication deteriorated into nit-picking and nagging.

"Vic, did you buy masking tape like I asked you to?"

"Yeah, it's around somewhere."

"But it's supposed to be here in the kitchen drawer. What good is it if it's not where I can find it?"

"I got it, I told you. I'm not responsible for keeping track of it. Maybe one of the kids used it."

"Well, why don't you tell your kids to ask first. Everything walks off and nothing gets returned!"

"Oh, so now it's my fault."

"Well, you're their father. They don't listen to me. But you just go have a beer and ignore the problems."

"And you make mountains out of molehills! Nag, nag, nag about everything. I'm sick of it."

"And I'm sick of you drinking all the time. You promised to stop and now you —"

"Quit telling me what to do! I can't even breathe without your permission! Do this!

Don't do that! I can drink a beer if I want to."

"One beer?"

By this time Vic would be angry and Laura would be in tears. "It felt like our life was out of control," she says, "but the more I would tell him what to do, the more he would drink. When he was drinking he picked on me, and that hurt a lot."

Later Vic might try to make things up by giving her a kiss, but, says Laura, "I didn't want him even to touch me when he was drinking. In the morning, however, he would be fine, so I soon learned that if I could just get him to go to sleep, things looked a lot better in the morning."

"We argued a lot over money," Vic interjects. It seemed to me she was always buying things whether we needed them or not. I wasn't about to let her spend all the money, so I would buy things I didn't need, also. Then we'd fight over who was to blame when there wasn't enough to pay our bills."

Laura knew her bossiness and nagging only made things worse, but she didn't know any other way to respond. "We got to the point where we couldn't agree on anything, no matter how trivial," she says. "But I was afraid he would leave me, so finally I'd say, 'You're right; I'm wrong.' "

But gradually Laura's fear turned to hate. "I no longer loved my husband," she says. "I wished I had never gotten married. In fact, I felt so tired that I just wanted to go to sleep and not wake up."

Each unhealed emotional wound primes us for revenge. We move from being hurt to blaming to hurting the other person. Around and around we go. These marital wars don't stop; they only reload. A break comes only when fatigue sets in. But it is not long until the next conflict bursts upon the scene.

Couples in this stage tend to believe they are trying to make life okay. They're making an effort; they're giving the other person suggestions. "If only my spouse would change!"

From then on the Miller's marriage started its slow, painful deterioration. For 12-1/2 years they mostly just put up with each other: she with his drinking and he with what seemed like her dominating control over their lives — especially his.

"I'm not sure why I drank so much," says Vic reflectively, "except it seemed a way to escape the duties of life. A couple of beers put life 'on hold,' and I could just enjoy the feeling that I had the world on a string, while truthfully, responsible people were passing me by and making something out of their lives."

Vic's drinking increased until, he admits, "I would even drink my breakfast sometimes. And when I was drinking, I was so busy feeling good with the numbing effects of alcohol that I easily ignored most of my responsibilities. If Laura asked me to wash the windows, hang a picture, or fix a faucet, even if it would only take a few minutes, I just wouldn't do it. Laura would have to do those things, or they didn't get done."

To Laura it felt as if Vic simply ignored her. "No matter what I would say, it didn't seem to bother him. It was as if he'd built a coat of armor around himself that couldn't be penetrated, and I was simply an object he owned. One time he told me he was going to put me inside a fence and keep me all to himself. But . . . I felt like I was already inside that fence."

As Vic's drinking and Laura's nagging increased, sexual intimacy decreased. "You don't care about me," she accused tearfully when he brought a can of beer to bed. "That can of beer is the only lover you need."

Vic sat on the edge of the bed finishing off the beer and said nothing.

"Please, Vic!" She hated to beg . . . but she was a healthy woman and had needs too.

But he just turned out the light and lay in silence with his back toward her.

"It's another woman, isn't it?" She could hardly say the words . . . but maybe that's why he didn't pay any attention to her anymore.

"Oh, shut up, Laura," Vic said, his voice muffled into his pillow. "Quit looking for problems where there aren't any. I just don't feel like it tonight."

Laura fought back tears of anger and frustration. When she was sure her voice was calm, she said into the darkness, "Well, if you don't want me, Vic, maybe I'll find someone who will."

It wasn't a serious threat . . . but Laura's loneliness and feelings of rejection were growing deeper and leaving her more vulnerable. When her father had surgery and needed someone to care for him for a couple weeks in California, Laura saw it as a chance to get away and get a grip on things. But while she was caring for her dad, she met a guy living in the same apartment building who was recently separated from his wife.

"We struck up a friendship which rather quickly became adultery," she says. "But it was so good to have someone say nice things about me again. For a little while I felt that maybe I wasn't so rotten after all."

The affair was over almost as soon as it had begun, though Laura wondered briefly if maybe it was a way out of her marriage. "But I didn't tell Vic — partly because I was afraid he didn't love me and wouldn't care anyway, and partly because I was afraid he would be so mad he would kill me."

Realizing the Miller marriage was in trouble, Laura's doctor recommended she go for counseling. "I went one time and was so afraid the counselor would find out about the other man that I didn't go again," Laura admits. "I guess I didn't want her to know that Vic wasn't the only person messing up our marriage. I certainly didn't want to take any of the blame. When she called to find out why I had cancelled the appointment, I lied and told her we had worked things out."

Never underestimate the addictiveness of misery. It's like a pair of worn-out shoes: they do little good, but at least they're familiar.

How we fear the unknown! We're afraid of the light that might reveal who we are. It's not that we're not hurting; it's just that the path to truth and health and new life is unfamiliar and thus terrifying.

But at this point Laura knew she needed help. Not only was her marriage in serious trouble, but it seemed her whole world was crumbling around her. It was October, but she barely saw the sharp colors of fall outlined against the Indiana sky. She decided to go to church with her brother and sister-in-law and, according to Laura, "That morning I found out what was missing in my life."

For the first time Laura understood what the term "born again" could mean. "God touched me in such a way that I felt like a newborn person. Somehow I knew God would forgive all my sins and I could start all over again. It was so real to me that I just didn't question it. But the first thing I said to the pastor was, 'You'll never get my husband to this altar.' "

However, Laura went home and told Vic about her conversion. Curious, he did go to church with her a few times, but then wouldn't go back. For a few Sundays she continued to ask if he'd go with her. "Leave me alone, Laura!" he said angrily. "You've just found something else to nag me about!"

Still, Vic admitted to some friends that there was a peace in their house that had never been there before. But . . . go to church? Not Vic Miller! What would the guys at the tool and die plant say if he got religion?

The heavy drinking continued all that

winter and spring. Now that all the kids were grown — Lucy was 19 and off to college — he didn't even make a pretense of staying sober. "He was taking a can of beer to bed every night," Laura remembers. "I didn't want to sleep with him anymore; I couldn't bear it when he touched me. If his arm fell across me during the night, it felt like it weighed a ton."

One hot July day Vic and Laura were arguing and insults were flying back and forth. Suddenly Laura snapped, "Do you want me to leave?"

"Yes! Just get your stuff and get out!"

So she did. After cooling off for four days at her mother's house, however, Laura went back home . . . but the arguing continued.

A few weeks later Vic — drunk as usual by early evening — announced he was going for a ride on his motorcycle.

"Don't, Vic," Laura begged. "You'll kill yourself."

"So whatta you care?" he mumbled.

"Look, I'll . . . I'll sleep with you tonight if you won't go." Almost as soon as she said the words, Laura regretted them. She hadn't been back in his bed since she walked out a few weeks ago. But — she couldn't let him go out on the road. It would be suicide.

Vic stood for a moment considering.

Then he got off the bike and went back into the house. True to her word, Laura shared his bed that night. But after he went to work the next morning she left him.

And this time she didn't go back.

Sometimes a few modest changes ("two aspirin, plenty of fluid, and rest") are all that are needed to regain one's health and vigor. But a major sickness requires drastic treatment. In this case, without intervention and strong therapy, the Millers' relationship was on the critical list and would soon be terminal.

Stopping a long-term pattern is often the only chance for success. Laura's ability to make a firm, radical decision — and to stick with it — was imperative. Rotten marriages need one or both persons to finally say, "Stop! Things have to change!" This is different than leaving the marriage. This kind of stopping only acknowledges the despair. Saying "stop" can lead to hope.

When Vic got home from work and realized that Laura had left, his first reaction was, "Now I'm really free! I can do as I please without having to answer to anyone." At last he was finally in control of his own situation.

After a week or two Laura called, wanting her pictures and things hanging on the walls. For a while Vic put her off by just not getting them down for her. But when he finally had to get to it, the thought of her never, ever coming back again was overwhelming.

"I suddenly felt as if I was caught in a flood," he recalls, "helplessly watching the shoreline — my marriage — slip further and further into the distance. The current was getting stronger and I didn't have the strength to swim against it to get back to the shore . . . which was looking better to me all the time."

Vic's newfound "freedom" soon turned into despair. "I realized then that I had really blown it and there didn't seem to be much I could do about it. Suddenly that old saying about not appreciating something until you don't have it anymore took on new meaning for me."

Laura, meanwhile, had moved in with her mother, was going to work every day, and to church three times a week. "I was at peace," she says. "Vic wasn't bothering me; I had put in an application for an apartment and was going to take care of myself."

But although she saved enough money to get a divorce, she never did file. Something was keeping her from it.

As summer faded into September, Vic

called Laura at her mother's house. "When are you coming home?" he asked.

"I'm not," she said firmly. And the argument was on.

Two days later, on Laura's birthday, Vic came to her work and left a birthday card for her. She had barely opened the card when he came back again and started arguing with her. Then, abruptly, he left.

"I was concerned about him," Laura says. "I called his shop at break time, but he hadn't returned to work that day and no one could find him. Then I got worried, so I called a neighbor and asked her to call me when he came home, which she did."

After work Laura went over to the house, walked in, and said, "Vic, I just wanted to know that you are okay." Then she left.

The next day Vic called and asked Laura to go out for dinner; she said, "Yes."

When she got in the car, Vic turned to her and said, "I've been talking to God."

Laura looked at her husband for a moment. "What have you been saying to Him?"

Vic swallowed and looked away from her gaze. "I asked God to forgive me."

Laura was so happy she wanted to laugh out loud. But instead she gave him a big hug.

"Where do you want to go eat?" he asked finally.

"Let's go . . . to my church," she said.

The church wasn't locked, but no one was inside. Together they walked to the front — where Laura had said to her pastor, "You'll never get my husband to this altar" — and knelt and prayed. Together they cried.

As the shadows deepened in the church, Vic looked at Laura sheepishly. "I poured all of my beer down the drain."

Her eyes widened. "You did?"

They continued to speak quietly, and suddenly they both realized something — for the first time in many years, they were talking without arguing.

One of the greatest joys of life can come when we move from lost to found. Vic had become so alone and disconnected. And yet, the blessings of God are always available.

Emotional and spiritual breakthroughs like Vic's and Laura's are like major surgery. They give us a chance to get well, to make a new beginning. But the "patient" (the marriage) still requires rehabilitation. This is the time for slow, consistent, hard work on rebuilding the relationship.

But Laura wasn't ready to go home yet. "Even though I believed that something important had happened to Vic, I was afraid he would start drinking again and I would lose the peace I had found," she says. "And . . . I still didn't love him, and I couldn't find anywhere in the Bible where God said I had to love him. About the only thing I knew for sure at that point was that God was in control of my life."

Laura's mother wasn't convinced Vic had really changed. "Don't go back to him," she pleaded. "What if you end up in the same old situation?"

"Mom," said Laura, "I'm positive that Vic is definitely a reborn person." But she too had her doubts. Would Vic be able to handle not drinking?

Let's go back to when Laura left and hear what had been happening from Vic's perspective:

"When it sank in that Laura wasn't coming back," he recalls, "I finally realized this was it — the bottom. Even more, I realized I was completely unable to help myself.

"I began thinking about the teachings of my youth and remembered that with God nothing is impossible. So I just asked God to take over my life completely. I made a firm and honest commitment to Him. And it was as if He picked me up and set me on my feet again. He broke the power of alcohol over me and — praise God! — until this day the desire has not returned."

When Vic shares this story he says, "I know that it will not work this way for everyone who has trouble with alcohol, and that many people will need AA or other treatment programs. God works in many different ways, and I pray that others will remain firm and committed to whatever works for them until they win the battle, because I know it can happen."

After pouring out all the beer in the house, almost immediately Vic began to feel better about himself and to see the world in a different light.

But this was not the end of their difficulties. "It was hard when Laura wasn't ready to trust my so-called commitment and wouldn't come back," he admits. "But for some reason I didn't feel hopeless. I felt as if a life raft had been dropped to me in the flood waters of despair by some unseen friend. It didn't completely solve my problem — but it did keep me afloat."

At 50 years of age, it wasn't easy for Vic to break a lifetime of habits and patterns. "I knew it would take all my strength and stamina to paddle that boat back to shore, but at least I had a boat. I decided I would do whatever it took to make the shore.

"Even more important, I determined in my mind that I would remain firm and committed to my new life of no alcohol whether Laura came back to me or not. I was going to take on my responsibilities as husband and father, factory worker, and citizen, and do my best to fulfill them."

Even with his new determination, when Vic went to see Laura, "It seemed as if the sky would cloud up and rain on my ball game," he says. "It didn't destroy the game but would keep postponing it. It felt like we would never get it settled."

Vic went to Laura's church and other places where he knew she would be, just to be with her. "While we were separated, I had been going roller skating a lot," says Laura. "It was something I liked to do but Vic never learned how. Well, all of a sudden this 50-year-old man showed up at the rink and put on skates — just to be where I was. It was as if God was saying, 'Laura, Vic is really trying, and he's your husband.'"

Laura was scared; she still didn't want to lose the peace she had found. She was first on the list now to get her own apartment. "I was frightened that I might make the wrong decision — whichever way I went," she recalls.

Now Laura realizes, "I guess I was running away from more than Vic. I was running away from marriage and the hard work

I knew it would take to ever make it work."

Marriage is a package deal. Getting what you want means giving all you can. We must first have a genuine desire to be a giving person. If we only act for what we can get out of it, then we are playing a power game. Manipulation and controlling behaviors set in, which breed defensiveness and resentment.

Rebuilding a marriage requires a genuine desire to work at relating. The bind is that non-relating avoids conflict — but produces loneliness. Relating makes intimacy possible — but requires serious communication, commitment, and effort.

Laura started reading her Bible a lot, desperately trying to find out what God wanted her to do. "I felt the only way I would ever go home would be if God picked me up and put me there!"

Vic was going to church and Bible study — both at Laura's church and his mother's church — and calling Laura every day. The interactions became very familiar:

"Please come home, Laura. I really want you home. I need you."

"I can't, Vic. I'm not ready."

"Well, I bought you a gift. Would you read it?"

"Sure, sure." Another Christian book he thinks will show me that God wants me home, she sighed.

"I've been talking to the minister at my mother's church," he went on. "Would you go with me so we can talk to him together?"

"Vic! I don't know this man, and it's none of his business."

"Well, think about it. I'd really like you to come with me."

Looking back at this time, Laura says, "It felt like every step I took I had a dog tugging at my pantleg trying to get my attention. And he just didn't give up!"

Finally Laura relented and agreed to attend his mother's church with Vic. But later she told him, "It's too big; I don't like it."

"Well, would you just come with me to talk with the minister?"

"All right! All right . . . just once."

But when they met with the minister, Laura didn't pull any punches. When he asked what she wanted in the relationship, she said stubbornly: "I want to get my own apartment."

"But if she does that, I'm afraid she'll never come home!" Vic protested.

To Laura's surprise, the minister helped Vic see that he needed to back off and give her some space. That was what she wanted to hear: Vic was finally going to leave her alone! They agreed to see each other on weekends, leaving five days every week when he wouldn't bother her.

As they left the minister's study, Vic said hopefully, "Would you go to Bible study with me tonight?"

Exasperated, Laura said, "No," went back to her mom's apartment, ate supper . . . and went to his Bible study. Vic's face lit up when she came in.

"A couple weeks later I was reading my Bible again," Laura relates. "I knew Vic had violated the biblical foundations of our marriage — and so had I. But God was telling me in so many ways that Vic was a new person, that all his sins were forgiven, and I should try to forgive him, too. I struggled with this until three o'clock in the morning. Finally I got up, put on my clothes, and went home to my husband."

As she stood in the doorway to their bedroom, she was crying and calling his name. Startled, Vic woke up and came to her.

"I have to come home," she said. They had been separated four months.

Vic tried to hug her, but Laura pulled away. "I was so frightened," she says. "I felt like I was in the middle of a tug-of-war. I had come home, but all the time I was telling God, 'I still won't love him!' "

But as the days wore on, Laura could hardly believe how patient Vic was with her. He went out of his way over and over again to please her, she admits. They tried several different churches hoping to find one they both liked. Finally Vic said he really would like to settle in his mother's church.

"Oh, great," muttered Laura, "just what I want — to go where that preacher knows all about us."

Reluctantly she agreed to go and, according to Laura, "We went into a Sunday school class and the topic was . . . marriage. Just what I wanted. Not only that, but guess who was teaching that class? Right. The pastor. The more I tried to avoid him, the more he seemed to be everywhere . . . and he knew all about me. I knew God was trying to tell me something, but I wasn't in a mood yet to listen."

The Millers' way of coping with the new adjustments in their marriage was to get involved in all kinds of church activities. "Doing these things together gradually began to draw us closer again," Laura admits. "Just the same, it took me two years to really begin to love Vic again."

Finally Laura decided she wanted this marriage to work not just because she sensed

God saying so, but because she really loved her husband.

"I finally had that gentle, loving man that I married back again."

Relationships are one of life's biggest mysteries. Why do we love? How do we love? Only God fully knows. Why do we hurt the ones we love? How can we be so destructive? Only God can understand and forgive.

But renewal and rebirth does happen — and this is one of life's biggest miracles.

Marriages can get back on track even when they require a total overhaul. Vic and Laura's marriage is a specific and personal example. But the themes are universal: stopping the cycle of destruction; personal responsibility; choosing to love as a decision.

Reflecting on the process of rebuilding a marriage after 14 years of alcoholic agony, Vic says, "The friends I lost when my life changed are not missed. The many people who have since entered my life have given a new meaning to the word friends. They honestly care and always respond when we need them. Their support and friendship make my life easier to live."

Laura agrees. "We still have problems, but we have learned that problems don't have to be forever and we aren't in it alone. We are surrounded by friends who make a difference.

"And," she adds, "when things seem to be getting more than we can handle — or even if we just need to share our struggles with someone — our pastor is always there, not necessarily to give advice, but to listen and to understand. We have learned that counseling is important to our marriage, and that asking for it is not a sign of weakness but of strength."

Vic also affirms that the support and counsel of the pastor was a real key in their reconciliation. "He helped me see that I first needed to straighten out my own life. I have to think things out carefully and do things in a mature, responsible way." Vic grins self-consciously. "These things don't come easily when you've been avoiding them for much of your life."

Most importantly, Vic says, their counselors have helped him become more aware of the needs and desires of his wife. "I have learned to say 'I love you' more often and really mean it. I always liked to hear those words, but seldom said them myself.

"I try not to take Laura for granted anymore. I hug her every chance I get and enjoy being close to her even without speaking." He shakes his head. "It seems we grow too soon old and too late smart. I'm thankful I have a second chance. I plan to take advantage of it!"

The Millers have gone out of their way to do things they both enjoy. "We've gotten so good at this that we have to schedule times to do the routine things — like grocery shopping or mowing the yard," laughs Vic, now in his sixties. But even beyond that, they are each learning to enjoy things the other person is interested in.

"For instance," Vic says, "I never did like shopping, but now I enjoy going shopping with Laura because it makes her happy. By the same token, she never did like ball games much, but now she goes along and enjoys seeing me enjoy them."

But Vic admits that learning to be more sensitive to Laura's needs is hard work. "I'm not accustomed to paying attention to small details, but I'm working on this. Sometimes it's like trying to hang on to a greased pig! I think I've got it, but let up for a minute and it slips away."

Learning how to communicate has been one of the biggest challenges. "Even though Laura is much more talkative than I am," Vic says, "both of us now try to allow the other person to finish statements before we start talking. That took some learning!"

"We've also learned that we don't have to yell and shout while arguing, and that it's okay to disagree," Laura adds. "Neither of us has to feel put down just because the other one doesn't agree. Sure, we still disagree, but the disagreements don't take nearly as much energy as they used to, they don't wake up as many people in the neighborhood — and when it's over we're still on speaking terms!" Vic laughs.

One of the most important things a couple can learn is: What helps our marriage and what makes it worse? When stress increases, conflict surfaces, and tensions mount, healthy couples turn to healthy options. Healthy options solve problems, maintain the teamwork, and move us through life's ups and downs.

Two years after Vic and Laura decided to rebuild their marriage, they also decided to try and help some of the many children who are in need of homes. "We started out participating in the Big Brother/Big Sister program," says Laura. "But one of the girls, 13 years old, begged us to take her home. So we became foster parents again."

For the next six years, the Millers cared for a total of 45 children — sometimes 9 at a time! "But we stuck to all girls, so that made it a little easier," Laura confesses.

"Many of these children were working with professional counselors," says Vic, "so we became involved in counseling as a whole family. This has been a supportive influence in our marriage! We learned so much more about each member of the family and became more aware of each person's needs.

"I not only learned how my wife felt, but why she felt that way. It gave me insights on things I was doing that hurt or aggravated her, even when I hadn't realized it. I love Laura, but I know now I will always have to be sensitive to her needs and desires if I want to keep our relationship healthy and growing."

The foster kids have dwindled, but the grandkids have multiplied. And the factory jobs have been exchanged for a joint business venture running a mobile home park.

But Vic has grown more poetic with the passing years. "Marriage to me is a lot like a boat," he says. "With little or no concern it will just drift aimlessly and never go anywhere. But with the desire and determination to make the marriage better comes a set of oars that can help guide it eventually to the right destination.

"Caring and supportive friends, pastors, and counselors, however, is like having a motor to propel the boat. At least for us, they have helped us keep on course and reach our destination so much easier than struggling every inch of the way by ourselves."

Chapter Four

The Power of Alcohol

by Stephen Wilke, Ph.D.

The downward cycles of marital despair and the upward cycles of marital hope have consistent themes. Lack of understanding, miscommunication, anger, blame, and distrust pockmark the road to brokenness. Awareness, honesty, mutual understanding, and forgiveness are building blocks for openness and healing.

When alcohol enters the marital scene a new layer of contamination is added. Let's review some of the ways alcohol fouls up marriage.

Deadens Pain

The reason we have nerve endings and feel pain is to protect us from destruction. If the nerve endings in our fingers didn't shoot with pain upon touching a hot object, we would burn our hands off. Feeling pain tells us something is wrong!

This is true of emotional pain as well as physical. Within a healthy relationship, communication between partners must be sensitive enough that pain can be readily communicated. "I'm hurt," "lonely," "disappointed," "frustrated," "tired" — and all the other emotional pains of life — must be felt and communicated.

The problem with alcohol is it deadens the senses and cuts off communication of feelings. When awareness of pain stops, communication doesn't follow, and as a result no response is made. While deep down inside we hope our spouse will nurture us, the pain is so covered over nobody even knows where it hurts — not even our spouse.

Without clear communication of the pain, the relationship is powerless to help. The hurting person soon sees the marriage as incapable of meeting emotional needs. The person goes outside the relationship with God and their spouse.

Hinders Healing

Another problem with alcohol is that it doesn't have anything constructive to offer. The alcoholic who drinks is like a person who needs to have an infected gallbladder removed, goes under anesthesia . . . but doesn't have the surgery! Alcohol is a pain killer, not a medicine. Persons caught up in drinking keep putting new bandages over infected wounds, all the time thinking they are "handling" the problem.

Demands Allegiance

Part of the challenge of being married is making yourself available to your spouse, listening, and being able to respond. A third problem with alcohol is that it is a controlling, self-absorbing drug which demands one's full attention. Like all addictions, alcohol becomes the be-all and end-all for the alcoholic's life. Alcohol wants no other loves before it — not God, spouse, or family. With alcohol people believe they need nothing else. They feel like they have it all, when in fact they have nothing.

Deceives What's Real

Another barometer of marital relationships is the way we feel physically. Healthy marriages provide a wide range of possibilities. Whether excited or peaceful or upset, the body's chemistry moves in tune with our emotions, which follow from the activity within the relationship.

Alcohol, however, is a chemical that dictates a predictable feeling which is disconnected from real emotional or relational events. Over time, the body believes it must have alcohol to function normally. This addiction messes up both psychological and physiological realities. What is in fact "killing the person" feels like it is sustaining them.

Overshadows Other Problems

Just as the total marriage suffers by the use of alcohol, a non-alcoholic spouse brings immaturities and imperfections into the relationship. However, the power of the drug is so great that little marital progress can happen until sobriety is maintained.

Steps Toward Wholeness

A marriage must be able to face challenges from the past, in the present, and with the future. If the physical body can become detoxified, work on the relationship can move forward. Persons who break the bonds of alcoholism often maintain a disciplined daily approach. To do this, the vast majority of recovering alcoholics use the basic concepts found in the Twelves Steps of Alcoholics Anonymous.

Likewise, just as the attitudes and actions of the alcoholic must change, so must the spouse's. A new way of being responsible for yourself and to your spouse must emerge. Both have pain; it must be heard. Both have manipulated; it must be forgiven. Both have needs; they must be met.

Alcoholism is serious business. It doesn't just go away. A marriage with alcoholism needs help. A combination of individual, marital, and group counseling is usually required.

However, like giving sight to the blind, recovering alcoholics and their spouses are able to see a whole new world.

The path toward new attitudes and actions can be long and difficult. Listed here are the Twelve Steps of Alcoholics Anonymous. They provide a structure or framework within which alcoholism can be successfully managed.

Twelve Steps of Alcoholics Anonymous

1. Admitted we were powerless over (alcohol) — that our lives had become unmanageable.

2. Came to believe that a Power greater than ourselves could restore us to sanity.

3. Made a decision to turn our will and our lives over to the care of God as we understood Him.

4. Made a searching and fearless moral inventory of ourselves.

5. Admitted to God, to ourselves, and to another human being, the exact nature of our wrongs.

6. Were entirely ready to have God remove all these defects of character.

7. Humbly asked Him to remove our shortcomings.

8. Made a list of all persons we had harmed, and became willing to make amends to them all.

9. Made direct amends to such people wherever possible, except when to do so would injure them or others.

10. Continued to take personal inventory, and when we were wrong, promptly admitted it.

11. Sought through prayer and meditation to improve our conscious contact with God as we understood Him, praying only for knowledge of His will for us and the power to carry that out.

12. Having had a spiritual awakening as the result of these steps, we tried to carry this message to alcoholics, and to practice these principles in all our affairs.[1]

To be effective, these steps must become

an integral part of one's life. As Christians use the twelve steps, their own faith and Christ's leading overlays and undergirds each step.

What can the Church do? Many are struggling with alcohol and other drugs. Many are struggling to make marriage satisfying. Seek out those who are struggling alone and need God's redeeming grace. Surround them in prayer and support them with fellowship. Stand ready to help along the way.

Farewell

The true stories you have read in this book are gifts of love. Love made them possible. Love caused them to be told so that you can learn to talk together again.

The Recovery of Hope movement is a network of couples who care about marriages. They care about hurting spouses because they've each been one. Let their stories be a gift of hope, an act of love, and a sacred trust that God's reconciling power will be available to you each day.

Notes

[1]*Alcoholics Anonymous* (New York, NY: Alcoholics Anonymous World Services, Inc., 1939, 1976).

What Is Recovery of Hope?

Recovery of Hope is a program for couples who are experiencing disillusionment in their marriages. Some may be contemplating divorce. The program recognizes that problems and disillusionment are normal in a marriage. However, many couples give up because they do not know what else to do.

Couples register for a three-hour session where a team of three alumni couples share their own experiences of disillusionment and the events and insights that created a spark of hope for them to attempt reconciliation. The new couples then consider their situation and how they are feeling about it. To aid in reaching a decision, a counselor will meet with the couple to help them tailor a plan to meet their needs. The reconciliation plan may include such things as counseling, meeting with a support group, programs for help in planning finances, parenting, and/or any other service which would be helpful.

ROH is based on sound psychological principles and basic spiritual values along with acceptance and support from volunteers and professionals. It provides a couple with time to review their marriage and make a decision about their future. While ROH is forthright in being "pro-marriage," participants' decisions are honored and respected.

If you feel like giving up on your marriage, you may wish to contact the Recovery of Hope Network. To find the program nearest you, call (800) 327-2590 in the U.S. and Canada.